Listen Up!

Listen Up!

FOSTERING MUSICIANSHIP THROUGH ACTIVE LISTENING

Brent M. Gault

OXFORD
UNIVERSITY PRESS

OXFORD
UNIVERSITY PRESS

Oxford University Press is a department of the University of Oxford. It furthers the University's objective of excellence in research, scholarship, and education by publishing worldwide. Oxford is a registered trade mark of Oxford University Press in the UK and certain other countries.

Published in the United States of America by Oxford University Press
198 Madison Avenue, New York, NY 10016, United States of America

Library of Congress Cataloging-in-Publication Data
Gault, Brent M., author.
Listen up!: fostering musicianship through active listening/Brent M. Gault.
pages cm
Includes bibliographical references.
ISBN 978-0-19-999051-1 (alk. paper)
1. School music—Instruction and study. 2. Music appreciation. I. Title.
MT930.G335 2016
372.87'044—dc23 2015035594

Contents

Acknowledgments

A project such as this one is only possible because of the assistance and support of many individuals. I would like to express my deepest gratitude to Norm Hirschy, Suzanne Ryan, and Richard Johnson at Oxford University Press. They have been encouraging and extremely patient as this book has taken shape. To my friends and colleagues at Indiana University and elsewhere, thank you for your ideas, suggestions, and opportunities to try these ideas out and refine them. I am especially grateful to Linda Noble and Beth Perdue Outland of the Indianapolis Symphony's Discovery Program and Madelyn Tan-Cohen, Luciano Pedota, and Christine Smith of the Ravinia Festival's Music Discovery Program for first providing the impetus for me to explore ways that children can experience pieces of music via multiple music channels.

I also want to thank the many students and teachers who have participated in courses and teacher education sessions with me. I feel so fortunate to be a part of such a vibrant community of musicians and educators and hope the ideas contained in this book are useful to you. Finally, thanks to my family for your love and encouragement.

About the Companion Website

www.oup.com/us/listenup

A companion website accompanies this book. On the site you will find PowerPoint presentations to accompany each of the lessons in the book. In addition, there are three sample videos on the site. Video 16.1 provides an example of one of the moves from Listening Experience 16 ("Hoe-Down" from *Rodeo*). Video 18.1 provides a model of one of the more difficult moves from Listening Experience 18 (Overture to *Ruslan and Ludmilla*). Video 19.1 provides a model of Listening Experience 19 ("Ecce Gratum" from *Carmina Burana*). All music can be located at the following Spotify playlist: https://open.spotify.com/user/bmichaelgault/playlist/4eowZklSm2Fru0lHrmxLLV.

Active Listening in the Music Classroom

Fostering Musicianship Through Active Listening: An Overview

One of the most prominent ways that we participate in music is through listening to it. It would be nearly impossible to go through an entire day without hearing some type of music, regardless of whether your career lies within or outside of the music profession.

Since listening to music is one of the primary ways that we interact with musical material, it makes sense that this behavior would be one focused on by music curricula in both elementary and secondary schools. We as music educators see the value of developing critical listening skills in a given music education setting, and school administrators and classroom teachers have also found value in developing this skill, possibly due to the fact that critical listening is transferrable to many areas of the curriculum and necessary for future success in a variety of fields.[1]

Listening experiences designed for an elementary music setting differ greatly according to the goals of the experience. This book focuses on developing active listening experiences for the elementary music setting. Through these experiences our students can foster music skills and reinforce music concepts actively while they listen to a variety of musical selections.

Active Listening: A Framework

At the elementary level, students commonly receive music instruction via a general music class that strives to develop multiple music behaviors (singing, listening, moving, creating, playing instruments) while also fostering a variety of music concepts (understanding of melody, harmony, rhythm, form, sociocultural aspects of music). Because music listening excerpts provide the opportunity to experience multiple concepts in one setting, they are a perfect vehicle for fostering musicianship and musical understanding in the elementary music classroom.

Many common approaches utilized in elementary music settings emphasize the importance of active experience with musical material as a forerunner to theoretical understanding. Teachers developing curricula around the philosophies of individuals like Emile Jaques-Dalcroze, Carl Orff, Zoltán Kodály, or Edwin Gordon seek to introduce new concepts and skills via some active musical channel. In these classrooms, singing, playing instruments, moving, chanting, and creating music all set the stage for the conceptual learning that is to follow. In a similar way, Jerome Bruner described a three-step process for representing

[1] Carlos Abril and Brent Gault, "The State of Music in the Secondary Schools: The Principal's Perspective," *Journal of Research in Music Education* 56, no. 1 (2008): 68–81; Carlos Abril and Brent Gault, "The State of Music in the Elementary School: The Principal's Perspective," *Journal of Research in Music Education* 54, no. 1 (2006): 6–20; Carlos Abril and Brent Gault, "Elementary Educators' Perceptions of Elementary General Music Instructional Goals," *Bulletin of the Council for Research in Music Education* 164 (2005): 61–70.

learning: enactive representation of learning that involves the use of active behaviors to illustrate given conceptual ideas; iconic representation that utilizes general pictures exemplifying a given conceptual idea; and symbolic association in which ideas are associated with specific symbol systems such as language or notation.[2]

Even though active approaches to music learning are a key component of curricular development in elementary general music settings, music listening instruction can often be a passive experience in which students listen to pieces without actively engaging in behaviors that would allow them to focus on the specific musical elements and ideas found within them. Since elementary school is a time in which students learn through active experience with their environment, listening lessons that engage students actively via specific musical behaviors allow them to develop a deeper connection with musical material. In addition, providing opportunities for students to engage aural, visual, and kinesthetic learning modes (as described by Barbe and Swassing[3]) ensures that a listening lesson will utilize the variety of strengths found in a given classroom while also allowing students to develop other learning modalities.

Strategies for Developing Active Listening Experiences

Designing active listening experiences requires the consideration of several factors that aid in the overall effectiveness of each experience.[4] First and foremost is the musical selection itself. Within all musical genres there is unique music, and finding those examples that are interesting, age-appropriate, and unique is critical if a music listening experience is going to be meaningful. Once a selection has been chosen, listening to that piece several times will reveal the prominent musical characteristics. Generally, these one or two characteristics are the ones most easily heard by students during a listening experience and can be utilized as the focus of that experience.

With the musical material selected, the focus then turns to the students and their previous experiences with the given musical material and the specific music behaviors that will be a part of the experience. It is important for us to know what prior learning our students bring to an experience and how that can be applied to a specific listening lesson so that they are able to use it as a vehicle for learning new information. In addition, we should assess our students' comfort level with performing specific musical behaviors (singing, moving, chanting) so that the listening experience begins by utilizing familiar musical behaviors before asking students to perform new and more challenging musical tasks.

With the knowledge of our students' musical skills and background in place, the final element is the learning experience itself. One consideration when designing such an experience would be to utilize aural, visual, and kinesthetic strategies to engage students actively as they listen. In order to help students have a successful encounter, the experience should begin with

[2] Patricia Shehan Campbell and Carol Scott Kassner, *Music in Childhood: From Preschool Through the Elementary Grades* (Boston, MA: Cengage Learning, 2013).

[3] Walter Barbe and Raymond Swassing, *Teaching Through Modality Strengths: Concepts and Practices* (Columbus, OH: Zaner-Bloser, 1979).

[4] Brent Gault, "Listen Up! Active Music Listening in the Elementary General Music Classroom," *Southwestern Musician* (February 2012): 62–65.

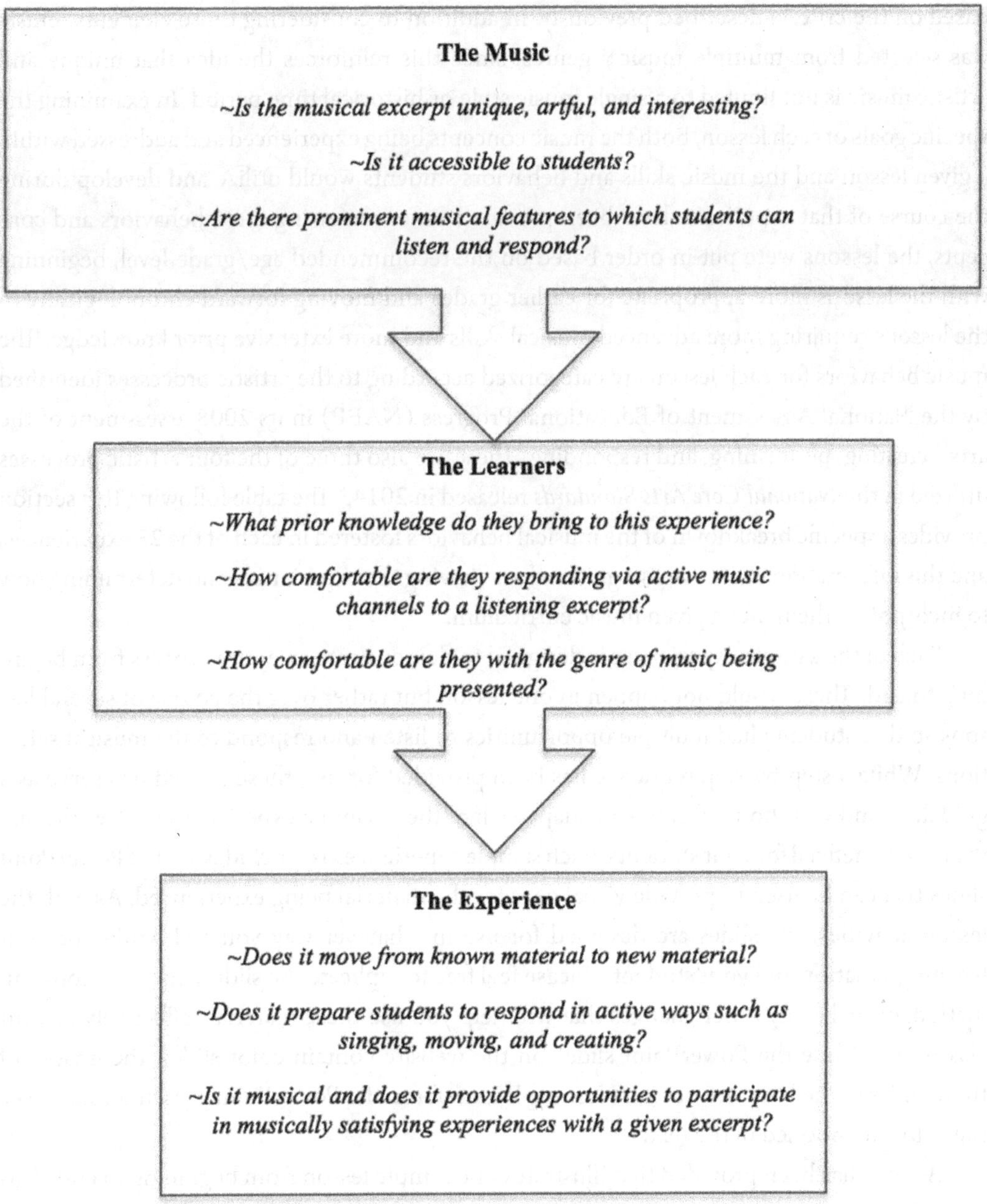

The Music

~Is the musical excerpt unique, artful, and interesting?

~Is it accessible to students?

~Are there prominent musical features to which students can listen and respond?

The Learners

~What prior knowledge do they bring to this experience?

~How comfortable are they responding via active music channels to a listening excerpt?

~How comfortable are they with the genre of music being presented?

The Experience

~Does it move from known material to new material?

~Does it prepare students to respond in active ways such as singing, moving, and creating?

~Is it musical and does it provide opportunities to participate in musically satisfying experiences with a given excerpt?

FIGURE 1 Framework for Developing Active Listening Experiences

known skills and concepts before introducing new or unusual material. In addition, musical behaviors should be meaningful and artful and give children a chance to foster a deeper connection to a musical selection. Figure 1 provides a summary of the framework utilized to create the listening excerpts in this book along with guiding questions the teacher can ask as he or she is developing an active musical experience for students.

Guidelines and Suggestions for Using the Sample Experiences

This book contains 23 sample lessons in which students can respond actively to selected pieces of music representing several different musical genres. The repertoire choices were made based on the criteria described previously. In addition to considering those elements, music was selected from multiple musical genres, since this reinforces the idea that unique and artistic music is not limited to a single music style or historical time period. In examining the specific goals of each lesson, both the music concepts being experienced and addressed within a given lesson and the music skills and behaviors students would utilize and develop during the course of that experience have been provided. After reviewing these behaviors and concepts, the lessons were put in order based on the recommended age/grade level, beginning with the lessons more appropriate for earlier grades and moving forward chronologically to the lessons requiring more advanced musical skills and more extensive prior knowledge. The music behaviors for each lesson are categorized according to the artistic processes identified by the National Assessment of Educational Progress (NAEP) in its 2008 assessment of the arts:[5] creating, performing, and responding. These are also three of the four artistic processes utilized in the *National Core Arts Standards* released in 2014.[6] The table following this section provides a specific breakdown of the musical behaviors fostered in each of the 23 experiences, and this information can serve as a guide when viewing the experiences and determining how to incorporate them into a given music curriculum.

Each of the sample experiences is designed to demonstrate an entire process from beginning to end. These would not happen in one lesson but rather over the course of several lessons so that students had multiple opportunities to listen and respond to the musical selections. While a step-by-step sequence has been provided for use, these procedures serve as a guideline, and you should feel free to adapt each of these sample experiences in ways that are the most beneficial for your students. Each sample experience also includes a set of PowerPoint slides that can be used to provide visual cues for the material being experienced. As with the lesson activities, the slides are designed for use in whatever way you feel works for your teaching situation and your students. Please feel free to replicate the slides, insert custom animation, or make any other changes that will help you use these materials effectively in your classroom. While the PowerPoint slides on the website contain color slides, the images of these slides in the book are not in color, so please refer to the PowerPoint presentations to see the colors mentioned in the text.

A video has been provided that illustrates one sample lesson from beginning to end. This video demonstrates a model for Listening Experience 19, "Ecce Gratum." Two additional brief videos have also been provided to illustrate some of the more complex hand-clapping sequences Listening Experience 16, "Hoe-Down," and Listening Experience 18, Overture to *Ruslan and Lyudmila.* I chose to only include these videos because my hope is that teachers can use the videos as an example of how they could use the materials within this book and then apply this information, along with their own knowledge of their students and their learning environments, to tailor the experiences for their unique situations.

---

[5] National Assessment Governing Board, *NAEP Arts Education Framework Project: 2008 Arts Education Assessment Framework* (Washington, DC: National Assessment Governing Board, 2008).

[6] *National Core Arts Standards* (Dover, DE: National Coalition for Core Arts Standards, 2014). Rights Administered by the State Education Agency Directors of Arts Education. Retrieved June 12, 2015 from: www.nationalcoreartsstandards.org. Retrieved June 12, 2015.

The specific performance tracks and artists that I utilized when creating these experiences have also been provided in the accompanying materials. For lessons in which changes in the sections of music are more difficult to hear, the timings of each formal section have been provided on the sample lesson plans. There are numerous recordings and interpretations available for many of these pieces, and you should feel free to locate and use a different recording of a given piece if you feel it is more appropriate for your situation and your students. The tracks I used while developing these experiences have been included on a Spotify playlist that can be accessed at the following link: http://open.spotify.com/user/bmichaelgault/playlist/4eowZklSm2Fru0lHrmxLLV.

Assessment of the musical behaviors utilized in these listening lessons can happen via observation of students as they participate in the experiences, small group participation in these experiences, or creative experiences such as asking students to develop new musical activities that match the musical characteristics of a given piece. In addition, these lessons can serve as springboards to lessons placing pieces within the cultural and historical context in which they were written or lessons introducing the composers and performers associated with each piece.

I hope that these materials will be valuable both in and of themselves and as a vehicle to provide ideas for developing your own listening experiences with other musical selections.

Listening Experiences

Musical Selections and Instructional Goals

Title	Composer or Performer	Musical Concepts or Experiences	Musical Skills or Behaviors	Suggested Age Level
1. "Skating" from *A Charlie Brown Christmas*	Vince Guaraldi Trio	Form Triple Meter	Creating movements to correspond with a given section of music Performing beat-related movements Performing movements corresponding to the contour of specific musical phrases Responding to formal sections through movement	Early childhood/ Kindergarten
2. "Walking Song" from *Acadian Songs and Dances*	Virgil Thompson	Form Simple Meter	Creating movements to accompany the "walking story" Performing to beat-related movements Responding to formal sections through movement	Early childhood/ Kindergarten
3. "Dwyer's Hornpipe" from *The Mad Buckgoat: Ancient Music of Ireland*	The Baltimore Consort (performer)	Form Simple Meter	Creating beat-related movements to correspond with the formal sections of the piece Performing beat-related movements Responding to formal sections through movement	Kindergarten–1st grade
4. "Den I Ronde 'Pour Quoy' " from *Danserye*	Tielman Susato	Form Simple Meter	Performing beat-related movements Responding to formal sections through movement	Kindergarten–1st grade
5. "Kathren Oggie" from *On the Banks of the Helicon*	The Baltimore Consort (performer)	Rhythmic Reading (Quarter Note, Two Eighth Notes, Quarter Rest) Form	Creating movements that illustrate the form of the piece Performing selected rhythmic patterns (reading from notation) with the musical selection Responding to formal sections through movement	2nd–3rd grades

(*Continued*)

Title	Composer or Performer	Musical Concepts or Experiences	Musical Skills or Behaviors	Suggested Age Level
6. "Laura Soave" from *Ancient Airs and Dances,* Suite No. 2	Ottorno Respighi	Musical Phrases Simple Meter	Creating movements to perform with musical phrases in the piece Performing beat-related movements Responding to and representing musical phrases via movement	Primary or intermediate grades (1st–3rd grades) (depending on whether nonlocomotor or locomotor movements are utilized)
7. "Humoresque," Op. 101, No. 7	Antonin Dvořák	Form Musical Phrasing Simple Meter	Performing beat- related movements Responding to the form of the piece through movement Responding to and representing musical phrases via movement	Intermediate grades (2nd–3rd grades)
8. "Radetsky March," Op. 228	Johann Strauss	Rhythmic Reading (Quarter Note, Two Eighth Notes) Form Simple Meter	Creating movements in groups representing specific formal sections of the piece Performing beat- related movements alone and in groups Performing selected rhythmic patterns (reading from notation) Responding to form through movement	Primary or intermediate grades (1st–3rd grades) (depending on whether nonlocomotor or locomotor movements are utilized)
9. "In the Hall of the Mountain King" from *Peer Gynt Suite* No. 1, Op. 46	Edvard Grieg	Form Rhythmic Reading (Quarter Note, Two Eighth Notes, Half Note)	Creating rhythmic patterns using text and rhythm syllables Creating movements to perform with rhythmic speech patterns Performing selected rhythmic patterns (reading from notation) both alone and with the musical selection Responding to formal sections through movement	Primary or intermediate grades (1st–3rd grades) (depending on whether nonlocomotor or locomotor movements are utilized)
10. "Finale" from the Overture to *William Tell*	Gioachino Rossini	Form Melody/Harmonic Progression	Creating movements to accompany one formal section of the piece Performing (singing) a melodic line corresponding to the harmonic progression of the formal sections of the piece Responding to the formal section of the piece through movement	Intermediate grades (2nd–4th grade)

Title	Composer or Performer	Musical Concepts or Experiences	Musical Skills or Behaviors	Suggested Age Level
11. "Menuetto" from Symphony No. 35 (Haffner) in D Major	Wolfgang Amadeus Mozart	Form Simple Triple Meter Melody/Harmonic Progression	Performing (singing) a melodic line corresponding to the harmonic progression of the first two formal sections of the piece Performing beat-related movements in simple triple meter Responding to form through movement	Intermediate or upper elementary grades (3rd–5th grades)
12. "Fiddle Faddle"	Leroy Anderson	Form Melody/Harmonic Progression	Creating locomotor movements to perform with one section of the piece Performing (singing) a melodic line to accompany one section of the piece Responding to the form through movement	Intermediate to upper elementary grades (3rd–5th grades)
13. "Entry of the Gladiators"	Julius Fucik	Rhythmic Reading and Improvisation (Quarter Note, Two Eighth Notes, Four Sixteenth Notes, One Eighth Note–Two Sixteenth Notes) Form Simple Meter	Creating rhythmic patterns using both "circus words" and rhythm syllables Performing selected rhythmic patterns (reading from notation) Responding to form and meter through movement	Upper elementary grades (4th–6th grades)
14. "Scène" from *Swan Lake Suite*	Piotr Ilyich Tchaikovsky	Rhythmic Reading (Quarter Note, Two Eighth Notes, Dotted Quarter Note–Eighth Note, Half Note) Musical Phrases Form	Creating movements to perform with musical phrases in the piece Performing selected rhythmic patterns (reading from notation and moving) for specific phrases of the piece Responding to the form through movement	Upper elementary grades (4th–6th grades)
15. "Fossils" from *Carnival of the Animals*	Camille Saint-Saëns	Rhythmic Reading (Quarter Note, Two Eighth Notes, Four Sixteenth Notes, Eighth Note–Two Sixteenth Notes) Rondo Form	Creating beat-related movements for specific formal sections of the piece Performing rhythmic patterns (reading from notation) for sections of the piece Responding to the form through movement	Upper elementary (4th–6th grades)

(Continued)

Title	Composer or Performer	Musical Concepts or Experiences	Musical Skills or Behaviors	Suggested Age Level
16. "Hoe-Down" from *Rodeo*	Aaron Copland	Rhythmic Reading (Quarter Note, Two Eighth Notes, Four Sixteenth Notes, One Eighth Note–Two Sixteenth Note, Two Sixteenth Notes–One Eighth Note) Form	Creating beat-related movements to perform with specific formal sections of the piece Performing rhythmic patterns (reading from notation) for sections of the piece Responding to the form through movement	Upper elementary (5th–6th grades)
17. "Berceuse" from *The Firebird Suite*	Igor Stravinsky	Melody/Minor Tonality Rhythmic Reading (Quarter Note, Two Eighth Notes, Half Note) Form Meter	Creating movements to correspond with the musical phrases of a specific section of the piece Performing (singing) patterns, a song, and a melodic ostinato in a minor tonality Performing rhythmic patterns (reading from notation) Responding to the meter of the piece through conducting Responding to the form of the piece through movement	Upper elementary (5th–6th grades)
18. Overture to *Ruslan and Lyudmila*	Mikhail Glinka	Rhythmic Reading (Quarter Note, Two Eighth Notes, Half Note, One Dotted Eighth Note–One Sixteenth Note) Form	Creating movements to perform with specific formal sections of the piece Performing rhythmic patterns (reading from notation) Responding to the form through movement	Upper elementary (4th –6th grades)
19. "Ecce Gratum" from *Carmina Burana*	Carl Orff	Melody/Major Tonality Rhythmic Reading (Quarter Note, Two Eighth Notes, Quarter Rest, Half Note) Form	Creating movements to accompany specific formal sections of the piece Performing (singing) melodic patterns, a melodic ostinato, and the melody of one section of the piece Responding to form through movement	Upper elementary (5th–6th grades)
20. "All You Need Is Love"	The Beatles	Meter Groupings (2, 3, and 4) Changing Meter	Performing movement and conducting to the changing meter throughout the piece Responding to meter through movement and conducting	Upper elementary (5th–6th grades)

Title	Composer or Performer	Musical Concepts or Experiences	Musical Skills or Behaviors	Suggested Age Level
21. "Unsquare Dance"	Dave Brubeck	Unusual Meter	Performing movement patterns and conducting patterns corresponding with possible note groupings in 7/8 meter Responding to the meter of the piece through movement and conducting	Upper elementary (5th–6th grades)
22. "1234"	Feist	Melody/Major Tonality Form	Creating movement to correspond with the form of the piece Performing (singing) melodic ostinati to accompany specific sections of the piece Responding to the form through singing and moving	Upper elementary (5th–6th grades)
23. "E-Pro"	Beck	Melody/Minor Tonality Reading Melodic Notation Reading Rhythmic Notation (Quarter Note, Two Eighth Notes, Four Sixteenth Notes, One Eighth Note-Two Sixteenth Notes, Two Sixteenth Notes–One Eighth Note, Eighth Rest, One Eighth Note) Form	Creating movements to correspond with the form of the piece Performing (singing and playing recorder) melodic ostinato for specific sections of the piece Performing rhythmic patterns (reading from notation) Responding to the form via singing, playing recorder and moving	Upper elementary (5th–6th grades)

Listen Up!

1 "SKATING"

LISTENING EXPERIENCE 1

Musical Selection:
"Skating" from *A Charlie Brown Christmas* by Vince Guaraldi (performed by Vince Guaraldi Trio, released in 1965; copyright 2006 Concord Music Group, Inc.)

Tonality:
C Major

Meter:
The piece is notated in 3/4 but is played at a quick tempo that creates a swing or "jazz waltz" feel (as if there is one large beat per measure divided into 3).

Musical Concepts Experienced/Addressed:
1. Form
2. Triple Meter

Musical Skills/Behaviors:
1. Creating movements to correspond to a given section of music
2. Performing beat-related movements
3. Performing movements that correspond to the contour of specific musical phrases
4. Responding to formal sections through movement

Age Level:
The activities described below would be excellent initial experiences with beat and form for younger students (early childhood/kindergarten) as a way to have them feel the beat and respond through movement to the form of a given piece.

Suggested Procedures:
(a) Initial Experience (Nonlocomotor):
- The teacher begins introducing movements via a story. "Boys and girls, it's a snowy day in the park. Pretend your hand is a balloon and move the balloon with me." The teacher will demonstrate possible balloon movements and the students will experiment. As the teacher does this, he or she will relate these movements to the balloon icon found on slide 1.
- The teacher will continue, "Now look up and see the snowflakes drifting in the wind. Make your snowflakes move around your space. Show me the different ways the snowflakes can

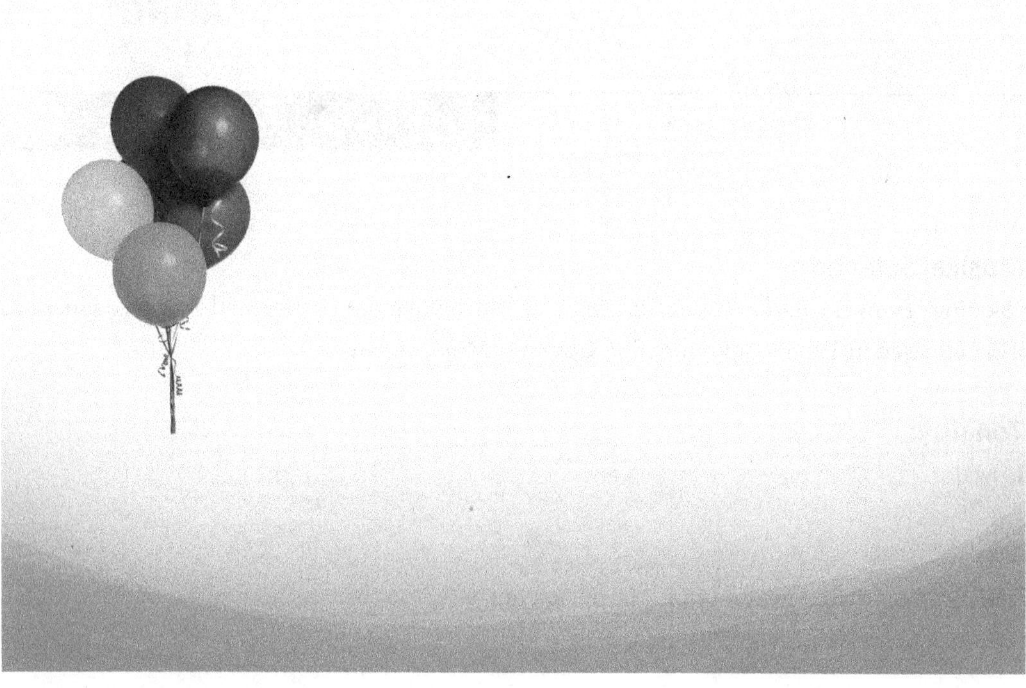

FIGURE 1.1 Listening Experience 1, Slide 1

move around you." Students will experiment with snowflake movements. As they move, the teacher will relate these movements to the snowflake picture on slide 2.

- The teacher continues, "Once the snowstorm ends, our balloons can come out and play again" Students will again follow the teacher's movements as the teacher relates these movements to the new balloon photo found on slide 3.
- The teacher will say, "Boys and girls, I have a piece of music that is perfect for moving balloons and snowflakes. The pictures you see are for the different sections of the music. Let's listen and move to the music (with our balloons during the balloon sections and our snowflakes during the snowflake sections). Follow my movements when we are balloons and move your snowflakes any way you like during the snowflake section."
- Students will listen and perform movements seated following the teacher's movements. The timing of sections is approximately:
  * First balloon section: Beginning to approximately 1:02
  * Snowflake section: 1:02–1:49
  * Final balloon section: 1:50–2:29

(b) More Advanced Experience (Locomotor):

- After experiencing the music and movement in the nonlocomotor version described above two to three times (in different class meetings), the teacher can have students experience locomotor movements. During the balloon sections, students will stand in place and follow either the teacher or a student leader. During the middle section (snowflakes), students can

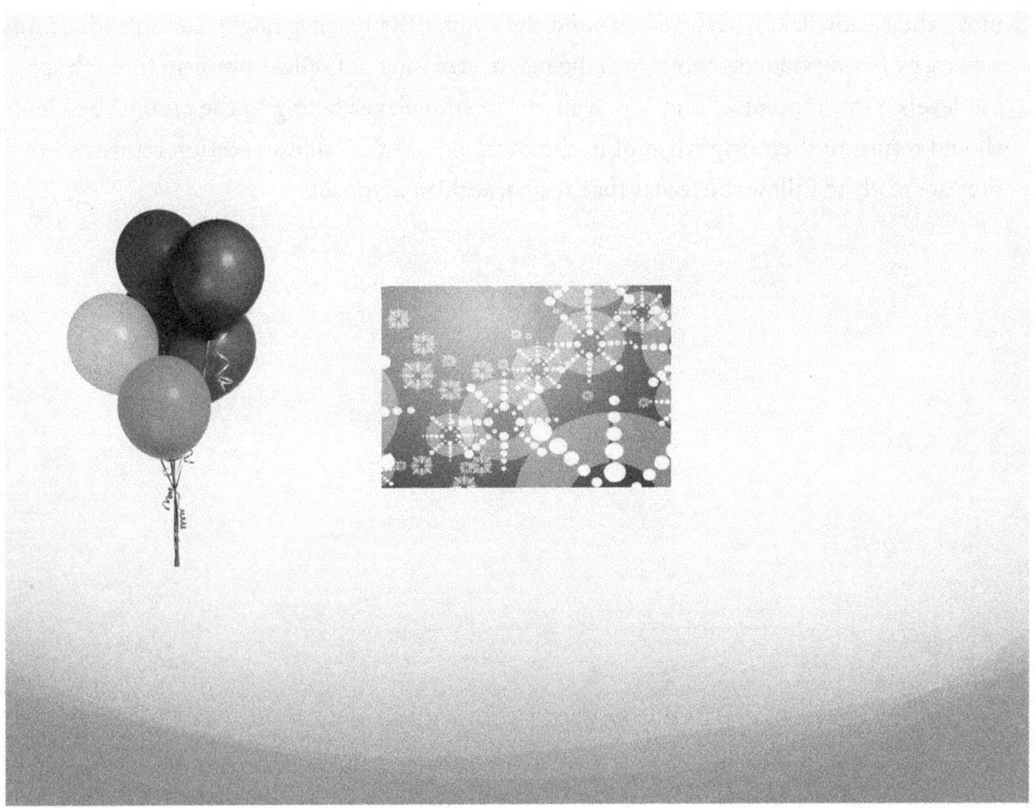

FIGURE 1.2 Listening Experience 1, Slide 2

FIGURE 1.3 Listening Experience 1, Slide 3

move their snowflakes anywhere around the room. The teacher might first introduce this activity by having students move with the piano, exploring not only movement through space but levels of movement as they try to show the snowflakes falling to the ground. Students should return to their original spot in the room before the balloon section returns so that they are ready to follow the leader for the final section of music.

2 "WALKING SONG"

LISTENING EXPERIENCE 2

Musical Selection:
"Walking Song" from *Acadian Songs and Dances* by Virgil Thompson (performed by Philharmonia Virtuosi from *Good Movie Music*, 2005, Essay Recordings)

Tonality:
F Major

Meter:
Simple Duple (4/4)

Musical Concepts Experienced/Addressed:
1. Form
2. Simple Duple Meter

Musical Skills/Behaviors:
1. Creating movements to accompany the "walking story"
2. Performing beat-related movements
3. Responding to formal sections through movement

Age Level:
As with the first experience, the activities suggested for this experience would be excellent initial encounters with beat and form for younger students (early childhood/kindergarten) as a way to have them feel the beat and respond through movement to the form of a given piece.

Suggested Procedures:
- The teacher prepares the movement to the music by incorporating all of the movements into a story and having the children act out the motions. The movements should reflect the musical events of the selection. For example, in "The Walking Song," the majority of the example utilizes a regular tempo. For this selection, any type of beat motion is appropriate.
- The teacher's story might suggest a walk in the park, where children can step a steady beat. Slide 1 represents one possible story idea.
- The images with the person walking could be points in which students step in place to the beat. The image of the sleeping face could be a time students sit down for a rest (this corresponds

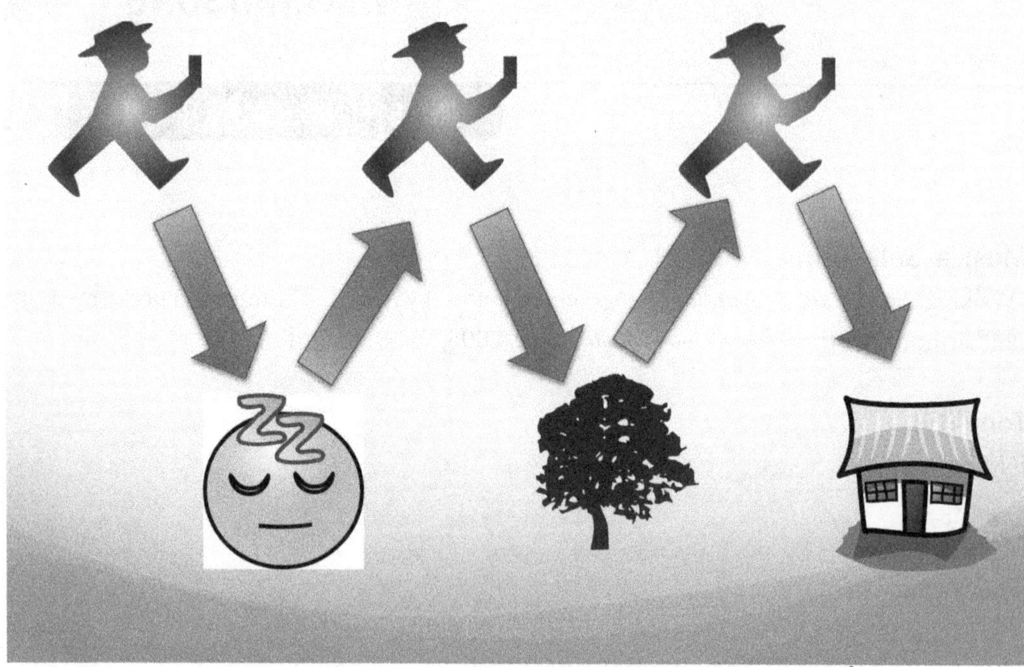

FIGURE 2.1 Listening Experience 2, Slide 1

with a slower section of the piece). The image of a tree would be a point where students could switch from stepping a beat to beat movements related to climbing a tree. The house at the end of the path represents making it home just in time for dinner.

- The purpose of incorporating the motions into a story before performing them with the musical example is so that the teacher may demonstrate and have students perform all of the movements before the music plays. Once the music begins, it is suggested that the teacher use as few words as possible to cue the children (referring to the PowerPoint slide), so that the focus is on the music rather than the teacher's instructions. The music corresponds with the images in the following way:
  First Walking Section (0:00–0:32)
  "Resting" Section (0:33–0:50)
  Second Walking Section (0:50–1:05)
  "Climbing a Tree" Section (1:05–1:13)
  Final Walking Section "Walking Back Home" (1:13–end)

"DWYER'S HORNPIPE" 3

LISTENING EXPERIENCE 3

Musical Selection:

"Dwyer's Hornpipe" from *The Mad Buckgoat: Ancient Music of Ireland* (performed by the Baltimore Consort, 1999, Dorian Recordings)

Tonality:

G Major

Meter:

Simple Duple (there are versions of this piece notated in both 2/4 and 4/4)

Musical Concepts Experienced/Addressed:

1. Form
2. Simple Duple Meter

Musical Skills/Behaviors:

1. Creating beat-related movements to correspond with the formal sections of the piece
2. Performing beat-related movements
3. Responding to formal sections through movement

Age Level:

The activities below would be appropriate for younger elementary students (kindergarten–1st grade) working with beat movement and representing form through movement. The initial nonlocomotor experience would be fairly simple, but the activity could grow in complexity as students create their own movements and also begin to move in locomotor ways to the steady beat.

Suggested Procedures:

(a) Initial Experience (Nonlocomotor):

- Students listen to the selection and follow the teacher's movements. Movements correspond with the formal sections of the piece. Possible movements could be:
  A (0:00–0:24): pat the beat on the lap
  B (0:25–0:49): move the beat to the stomach
  (After the initial themes, A and B alternate until the end of the piece.)
- The teacher shows a visual of the form (using pictures to represent each section) (slide 1).

Listen and Follow Me!

FIGURE 3.1 Listening Experience 3, Slide 1

How Can We Keep the Beat ?

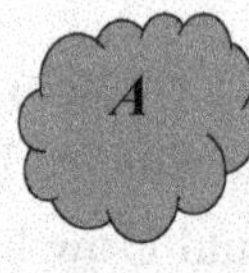

FIGURE 3.2 Listening Experience 3, Slide 2

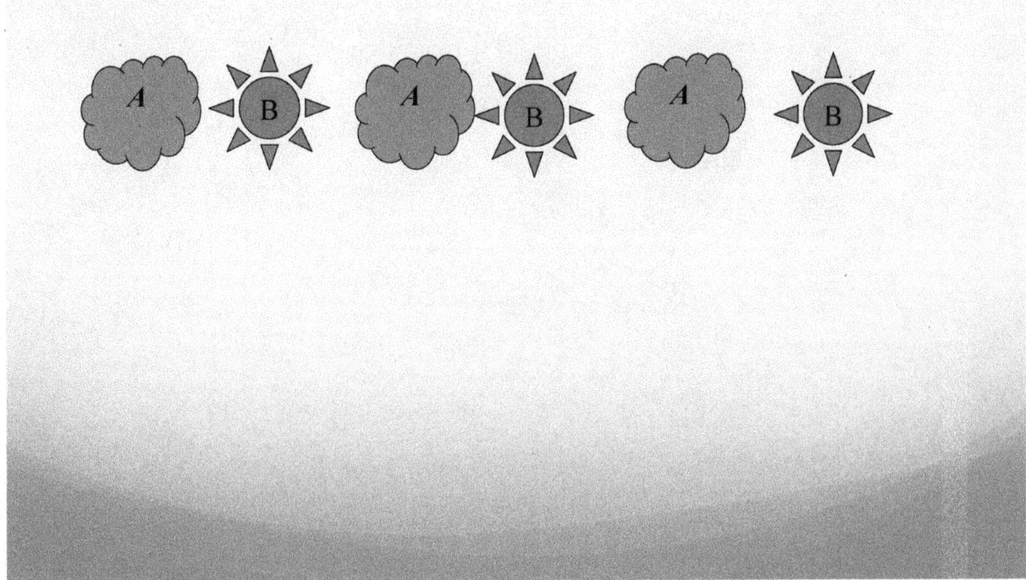

FIGURE 3.3 Listening Experience 3, Slide 3

- The teacher asks students to create nonlocomotor beat movements to accompany the two sections of music (slide 2).
- Students will listen and perform their own movements for A and B sections of the music (slide 3).

(b) More Advanced Experience:

- Once students are comfortable, they can create locomotor movements for each section of the piece and move as they listen to the piece.

4

"DEN I RONDE 'POUR QUOY'"

LISTENING EXPERIENCE 4

Musical Selection:
"Den I Ronde 'Pour Quoy' " from *Danserye* (1551) by Tielman Susato (performed by the New London Consort and Phillip Pickett, 1993, Decca Music Group Limited)

Tonality:
G Minor

Meter:
Simple Duple (4/4)

Musical Concepts Experienced/Addressed:
1. Form
2. Simple Meter

Musical Skills/Behaviors:
1. Performing beat-related movements
2. Responding to formal sections through movement

Age Level:
The activities below would be appropriate for younger elementary students (kindergarten–1st grade) working with beat movement and representing form through movement. The initial nonlocomotor experience would be fairly simple, but the addition of movement through space and with partners would pose more challenges and be appropriate after students gain comfort with the music and the movements in the nonlocomotor format.

Suggested Procedures:
(a) Initial Experience (Nonlocomotor):
- Students listen to the selection as they mirror nonlocomotor (stationary) movements with the teacher. Movements correspond to the three major sections of the piece. As students mirror the teacher's movements, the teacher will draw students' attention to slide 1 demonstrating the different formal sections.
- Possible movements could be:
  * A (Red Heptagon): alternating pats to the beat on each leg
  * B (Yellow Happy Face): 4-beat pattern two times (pat-clap-right hand out-left hand out)

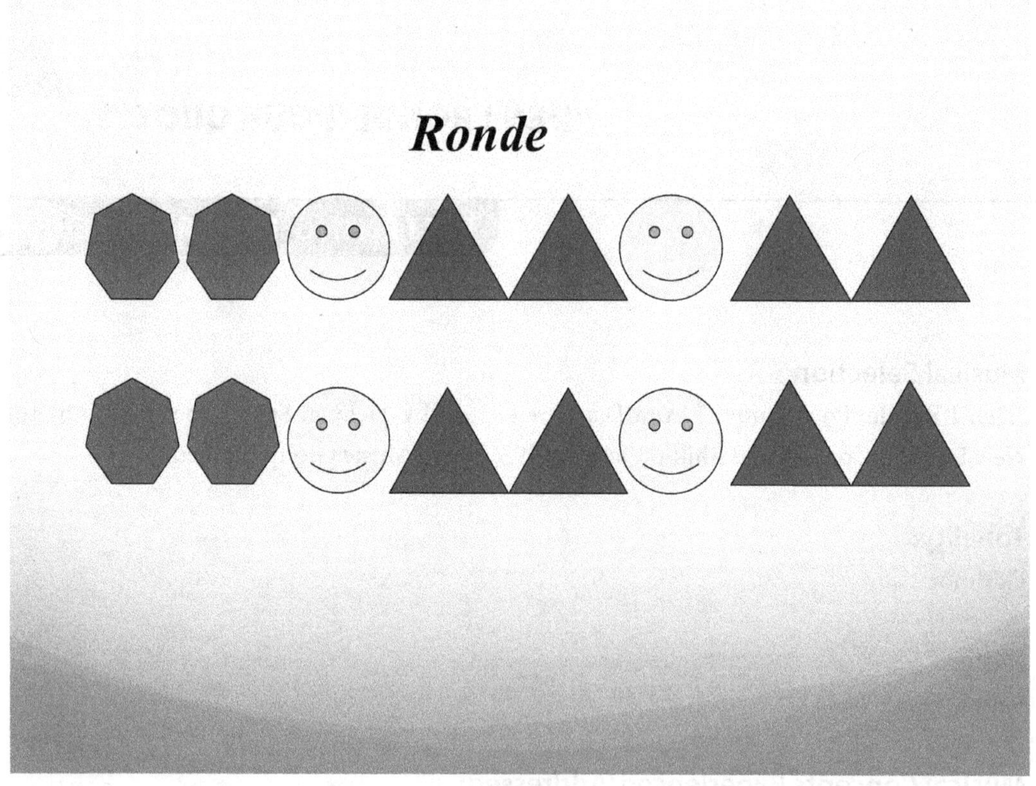

FIGURE 4.1 Listening Experience 4, Slide 1

* C (Blue Triangle): beat movement with palms out (4 beats with one hand then 4 beats with the other hand)

– The teacher will provide information about the type of piece ("Ronde" or Round Dance). The teacher will ask students to provide new ideas for ways to keep the beat during each formal section, and students will listen and perform again (during different class sessions).

(b) More Advanced Experience (Locomotor):

– After listening and performing the initial movements described above, the teacher will review the definition of "Ronde" and have students stand and find space to move. The teacher will provide locomotor movements that correspond to the sections of the piece:
  * A (Red Heptagon): Walk 8 beats. During the repeat of the A section, students will find a partner by the end of the 8 beats.
  * B (Yellow Happy Face): Face a partner and perform the 4-beat pattern (pat-clap-right hand out-left hand out) with partner
  * C (Blue Triangle): 4-beat turn while touching palms with partner; 4-beat turn while touching opposite palms with partner

– Student will perform with music.

– Once students are comfortable with the music and the form, they can develop new locomotor movements to perform with the sections of music.

– Form:
A: (0:00-0:11)
A: (0:11-0:18)
B: (0:18-0:25)
C: (0:25-0:33)
C: (0:33-0:40)
B: (0:40-0:47)
C: (0:47-0:55)
C: (0:55-1:02)

The entire piece repeats beginning at 1:02.

"KATHREN OGGIE" 5

Musical Selection:
"Kathren Oggie" from *On the Banks of the Helicon: Early Music of Scotland* (performed by the Baltimore Consort, 1990, Sono Luminus)

Tonality:
G Dorian

Meter:
Simple Duple (4/4)

Musical Concepts Experienced/Addressed:
1. Form
2. Rhythmic Reading (Quarter Note, Two Eighth Notes, Quarter Rest)

Musical Skills/Behaviors:
1. Creating movements that illustrate the form of the piece
2. Performing selected rhythmic patterns (reading from notation) with the musical selection
3. Responding to formal sections through movement

Age Level:
The nonlocomotor version of this experience is appropriate as a way to review simple rhythms in primary grades. The locomotor activities might be more appropriate a bit later (2nd–3rd grades).

Suggested Procedures:
- Students begin by echo speaking and reviewing simple rhythms as they view slide 1.
- After reviewing the rhythms on slide 1, students will read and speak the rhythms on slides 2 and 3.
- Students will view slide 4, showing the form of "Kathren Oggie." Students will listen to the piece and tap the rhythmic pattern on slide 2 for the A sections and the rhythmic pattern for slide 3 during the B sections. Slides 5–15 have these patterns in order based on the form of the piece.

FIGURE 5.1 Listening Experience 5, Slide 1

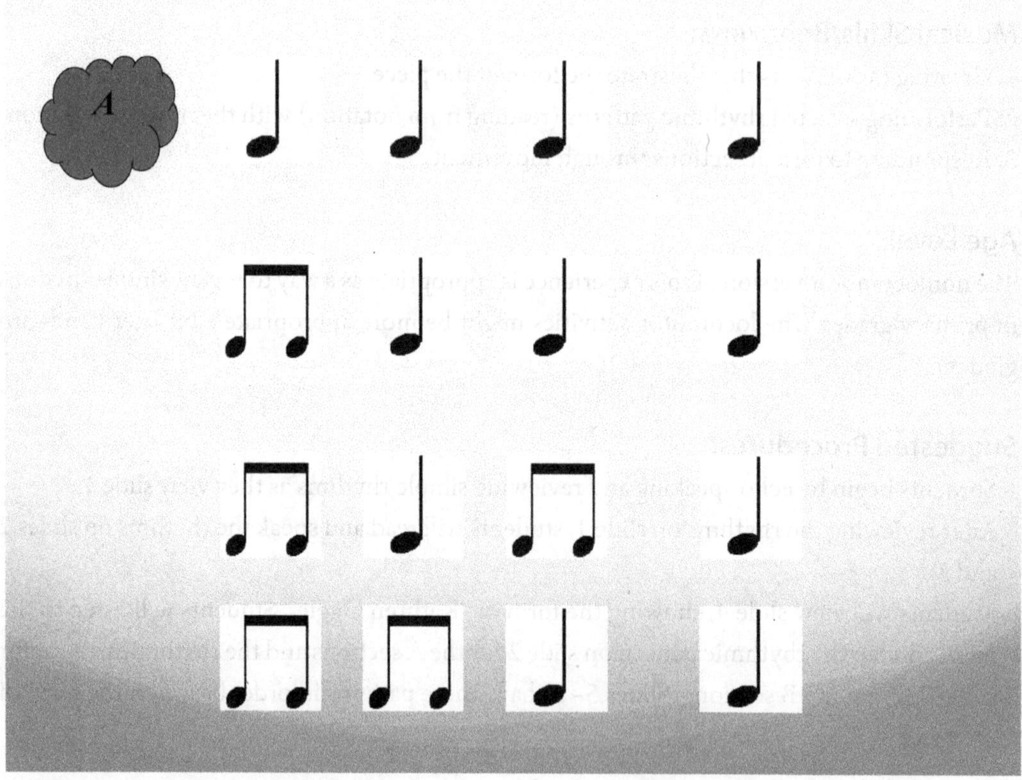

FIGURE 5.2 Listening Experience 5, Slide 2

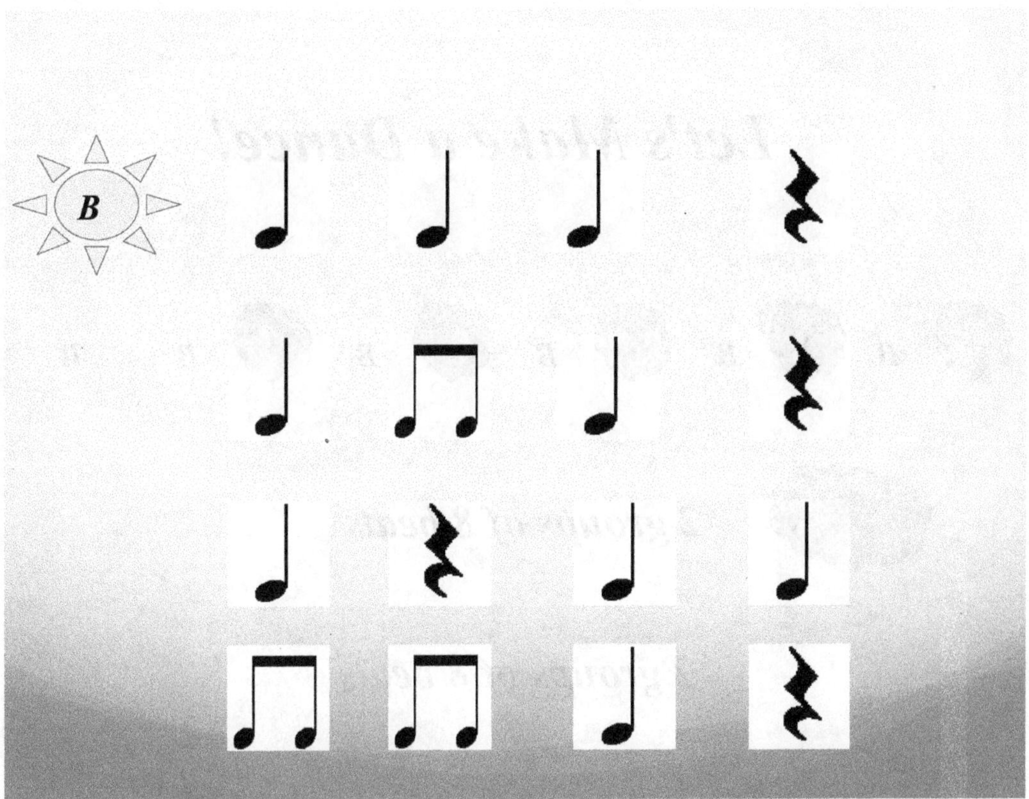

FIGURE 5.3 Listening Experience 5, Slide 3

FIGURE 5.4 Listening Experience 5, Slide 4

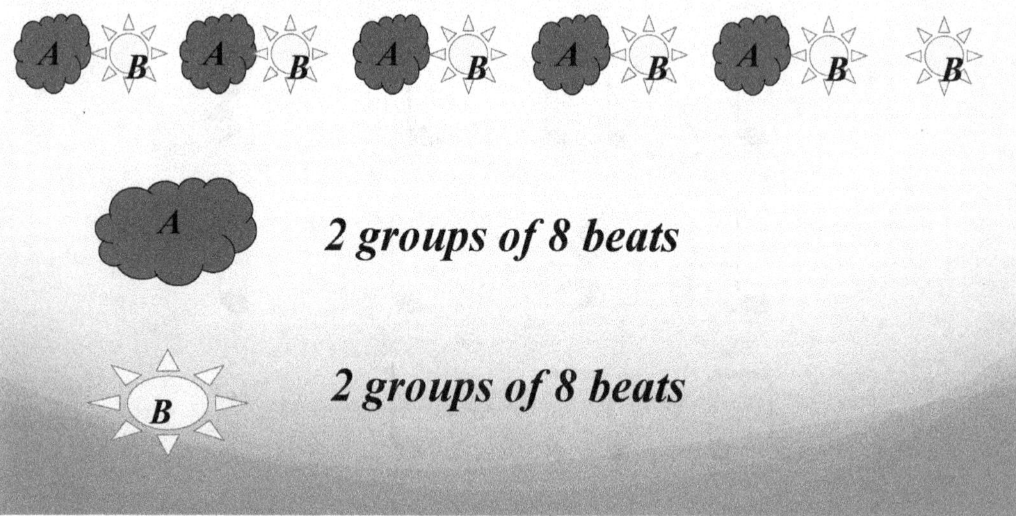

FIGURE 5.5 Listening Experience 5, Slide 5

- As a more complex experience (now that students can listen and tap), students can stand and step the rhythmic patterns for A and B. After this, students can step the rhythms as they listen to the piece.
- After working with the piece through the use of the rhythmic patterns, students can view slide 16. Instead of stepping the rhythms for each sections, students can create a dance that corresponds to the form of the song, creating two 8-beat motions to perform with A and two 8-beat motions to perform with B.
- Extension activities for this experience would include creating dances in various formations (circle, longways set in which there are two lines of people facing a partner) or composing 16-beat rhythmic patterns to perform with A and B.

"LAURA SOAVE"* 6

LISTENING EXPERIENCE 6

Musical Selection:

"Laura Soave" from *Ancient Airs and Dances,* Suite No. 2 by Ottorno Respighi (performed by Rico Saccani and the National Symphony Orchestra of Ireland, 1996, Naxos)

Tonality:

D Major

Meter:

Simple Duple (4/4)

Musical Concepts Experienced/Addressed:

1. Musical Phrasing
2. Simple Duple Meter

Musical Skills/Behaviors:

1. Creating movements representing the musical phrases of the piece
2. Performing beat-related movements
3. Responding to and representing musical phrases via movement

Age Level:

This particular experience begins fairly simply using nonlocomotor movements and could be done at the early elementary age level (1st grade, for example). As the activities become more advanced (adding movement and then moving with objects), students would need comfort moving to a steady beat, being creative with movement, and moving with objects. This could happen in the same grade level, or this excerpt could return at a later grade (2nd or 3rd) as an opportunity to move in more complex ways with musical phrases.

Suggested Procedures:

(a) Initial Experience (Nonlocomotor):

- Students listen and follow the teacher's beat pattern. The pattern will correspond to the number of beats in each phrase of music. One possible idea would be: pat-pat-pat-pat-pat-pat-pat-clap (it is suggested that the pats and claps be as silent and smooth as possible so they correspond with the legato style of the music).

---

* This experience uses the first 1:20 of the piece.

- The teacher will ask the students to describe the pattern (a group of 8 beats in which all movements are the same except the last one). Students will create other nonlocomotor movements to perform with the music and do this again as they listen.

(b) Moving to Music Phrases:

- Once students have had opportunities to move in nonlcomotor ways to the form of the piece, the teacher will introduce a new pattern: step-step-step-step-step-step-step-turn. Students will stand and "move" the phrases as they listen.
- Since the piece conveys a "stately" feel, the teacher will then have students move as if they are "royalty." Rather than turning on the last beat of the pattern, students will use that beat to give a royal nod of the head to another person. As a result, the pattern that is repeated with the phrases is: step-step-step-step-step-step-step-nod.

(c) Moving with Objects:

- Students will form a circle with one to two individuals in the middle. Students in the middle of the circle are given an object (e.g., ball, scarf) that represents the musical phrase. These students will step for 7 beats and then "pass the phrase" on beat 8. The person receiving the phrase will take the object and begin stepping on the new phrase (passing on beat 8). This continues until the piece is over.
- Students create statues around the room. One person is given a ball, scarf, or other item to indicate they are "it." This person walks around the room and passes the object to another person on beat 8. The new person is "it" and now moves for 8 beats, passing to another person on beat 8. Once the object is passed, the person who releases the object must freeze in place as a statue (only people holding the object can move). The game continues with the music. For large classes, more than one person can be "it."

"HUMORESQUE," OP. 101, NO.7 7

LISTENING EXPERIENCE 7

Musical Selection:
"Humoresque," Op. 101, No. 7 by Antonin Dvořák (from *99 Must-Own Classical Music Collection*, performed by Hans Kalafusz, violin, and Klaus von Vilemann, piano; 2013, R.B. Puddin)

Tonality:
G Major

Meter:
Simple Duple (2/4)

Musical Concepts Experienced/Addressed:
1. Form
2. Musical Phrasing
3. Simple Duple Meter (2/4)

Musical Skills/Behaviors:
1. Performing beat-related movements
2. Responding to the form of the piece through movement
3. Responding to and representing musical phrases via movement

Age Level:
The nonlocomotor version of this activity is fairly simple and could be done in early elementary school. As students begin to move through space and move with objects, the level of difficulty increases and the activity might be more appropriate for mid-level elementary students (2nd or 3rd grades).

Suggested Procedures:
– Students will follow the teacher's movements as they view slide 1.
– Students will listen to the piece as they imitate the teacher's nonlocomotor movements:
  A: pat-pat-pat-pat/pat-pat-pat-pat/pat-pat-pat-pat/arms out for 4 beats
  pat-pat-pat-pat/pat-pat-pat-pat/pat-pat-pat-pat/arms out for 4 beats
  B: sway arms from side to side to the beat
  C: pat-clap-snap-clap (8 times)

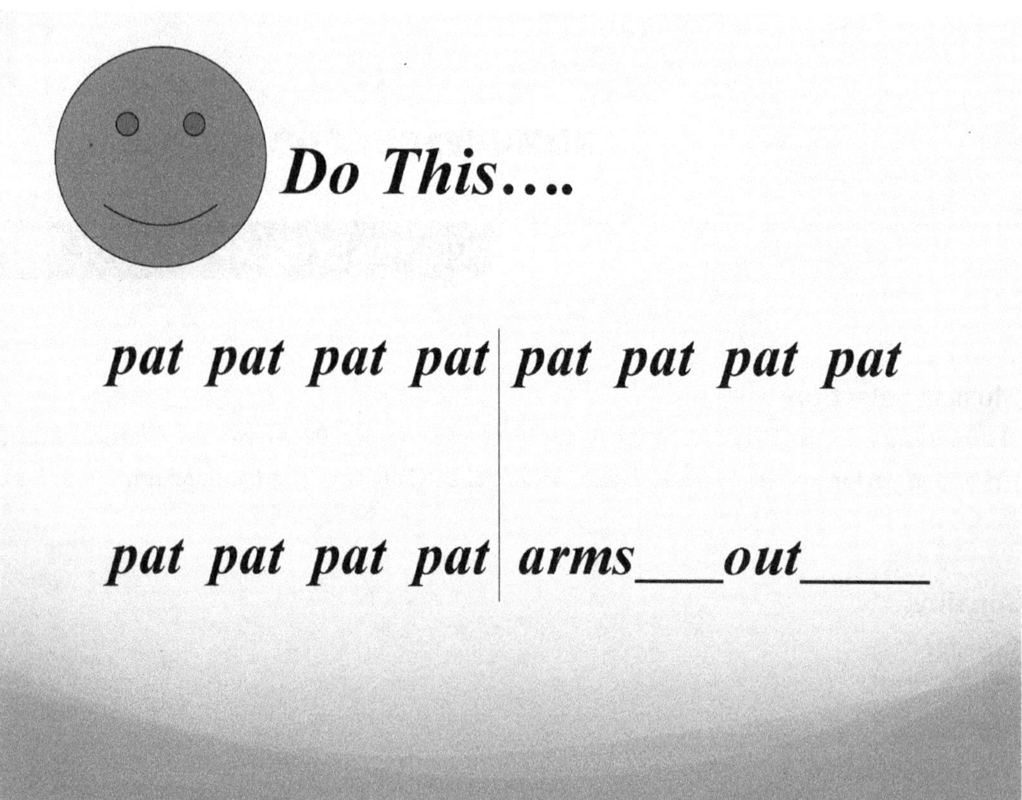

FIGURE 7.1 Listening Experience 7, Slide 1

FIGURE 7.2 Listening Experience 7, Slide 2

Form: A-A-B-A-C-C-A-B (Each section is 32 beats long [8 measures of 4])

- Students will view slide 2, and the teacher will relate the movements to the shapes on the slide (A movement = Happy Face; B movement = Heart; C movement = Storm Cloud).
- Students will listen and perform movements again as they view the visual.
- Students stand and listen again, but with the following movement changes:

  A (Happy Face): step-step-step-step/step-step-step-step/step-step-step-step/arms out for 4 beats

  B (Heart): sway arms from side to side to the beat

  C (Storm Clouds): conduct (in 4)
- Students form a circle and listen again. During the A section, students go back to using the nonlocomotor movement (patting and arms out). One or two students are given an object such as a ball or a scarf. These students step inside the circle during the first three measures of A and then pass the object on the 4th measure:

  A: step-step-step-step/step-step-step-step/step-step-step-step/pass for 4 beats
- Students move to scattered space and repeat the activity with students who have objects movement and passing during the A section.

8 "RADETSKY MARCH," OP. 228

LISTENING EXPERIENCE 8

Musical Selection:
"Radetsky March," Op. 228 by Johann Strauss (from *Great Marches* performed by Leonard Bernstein and The New York Philharmonic, 1997, Sony Classical)

Tonality:
D Major

Meter:
Simple Duple (4/4)

Musical Concepts Experienced/Addressed:
1. Form
2. Rhythmic Reading (Quarter Note, Two Eighth Notes)
3. Simple Duple Meter (4/4)

Musical Skills/Behaviors:
1. Creating movements in groups representing specific formal sections of the piece
2. Performing beat-related movements alone and in groups
3. Performing selected rhythmic patterns (reading from notation)
4. Responding to form through movement

Age Level:
This activity would be appropriate for use with primary grades (1st–2nd grades) as a way of reinforcing pulse and form while also utilizing simple rhythmic patterns that students could read and perform. The more advanced locomotor experience would be more appropriate for intermediate grades (3rd, for example).

Suggested Procedures:
(a) Initial Experience (Nonlocomotor):
- Students begin by learning and speaking a rhyme that will become a second part to be added to the A section of the march (slide 1).
- Once students learn the chant, they will internalize the words as they tap the rhythm of the text with the A section of "Radetsky March" (slide 2) (0:00–0:22). There is an 8-beat introduction before the A section begins.

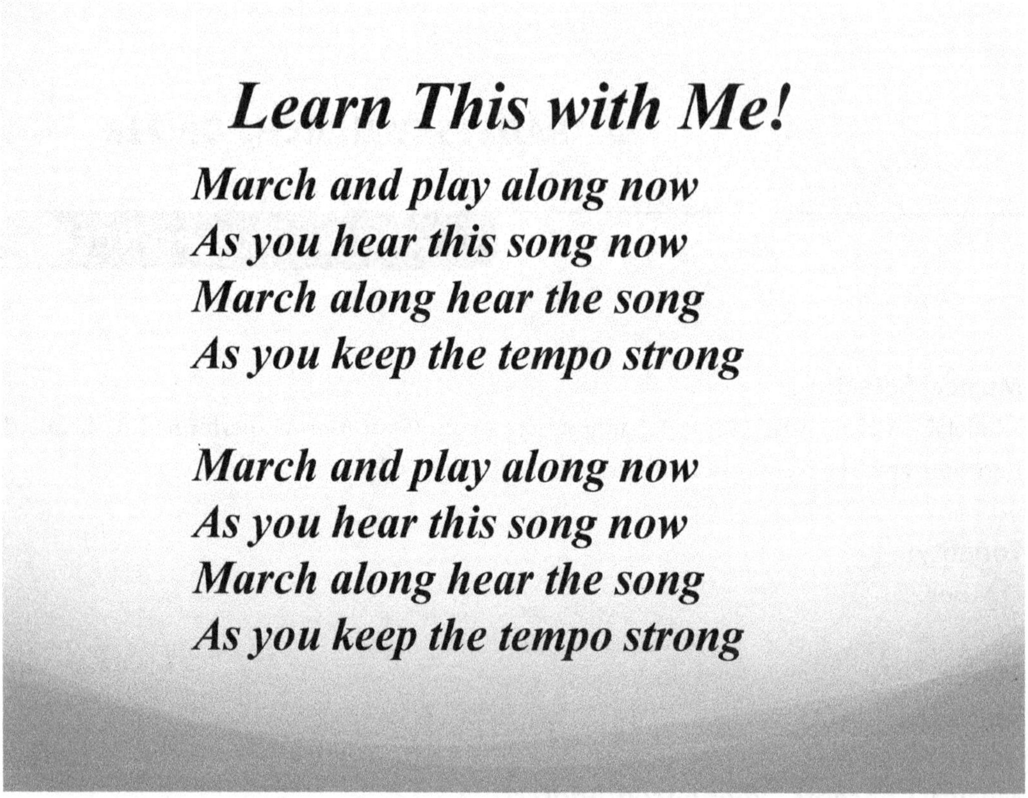

Learn This with Me!

March and play along now
As you hear this song now
March along hear the song
As you keep the tempo strong

March and play along now
As you hear this song now
March along hear the song
As you keep the tempo strong

FIGURE 8.1 Listening Experience 8, Slide 1

- Once students can internalize the words of the rhyme and tap the rhythm of the text, the teacher can show the rhythm of the rhyme in notation (slide 3). Students can speak the rhythm on text or rhythm syllables and listen to the A section again as they tap and view the notation (slide 4).
- The teacher will show students a visual of the form of the piece that includes movements for each formal section (slides 5 and 6):
  For the A section: tap the rhythm of the rhyme
  For the B section: pat—clap—hands out—clap
  For the C section: conduct
  For the C' section: stand and conduct
- Students will listen to "Radetsky March" as they perform nonlocomotor movements. Slide 7 provides a visual of the entire form of the piece.

(b) Formal Sections and Timings:

Introduction (0:00–0:04)
A (0:04–0:22)
B (0:22–0:40)
A (0:41–0:58)
Bridge (0:59–1:02)
C (1:03–1:20)
C' (1:21–1:38)
C' (1:39–1:57)

Now Read It this Way!

FIGURE 8.2 Listening Experience 8, Slide 3

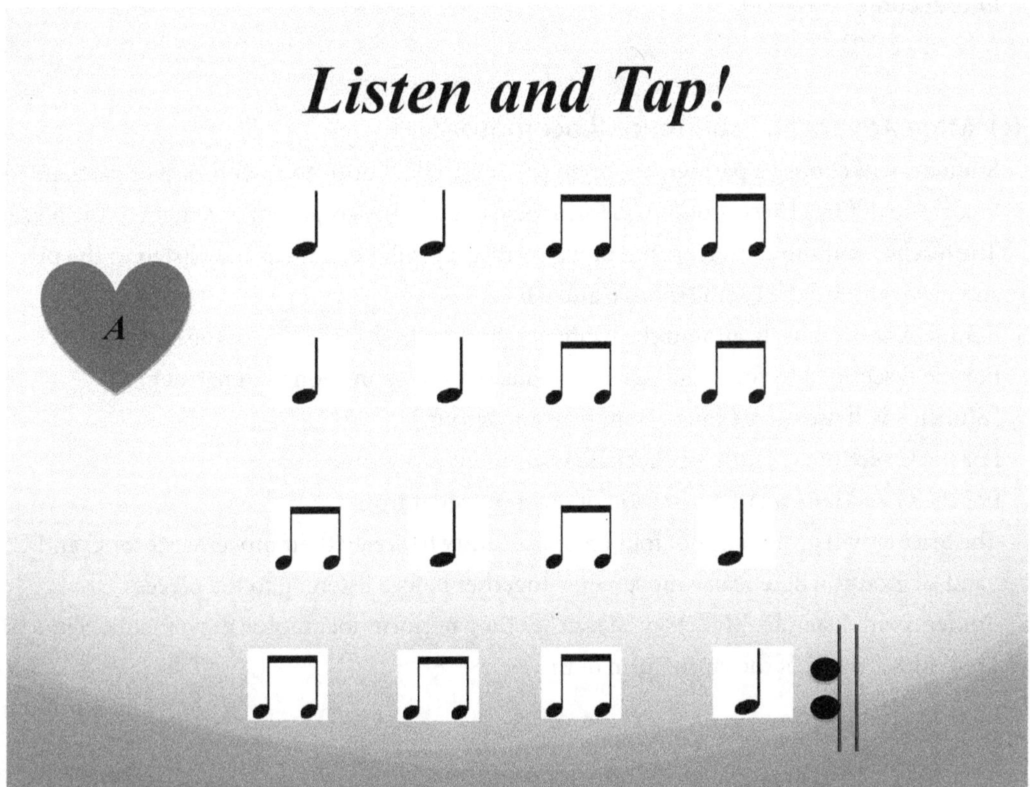

Listen and Tap!
A

FIGURE 8.3 Listening Experience 8, Slide 4

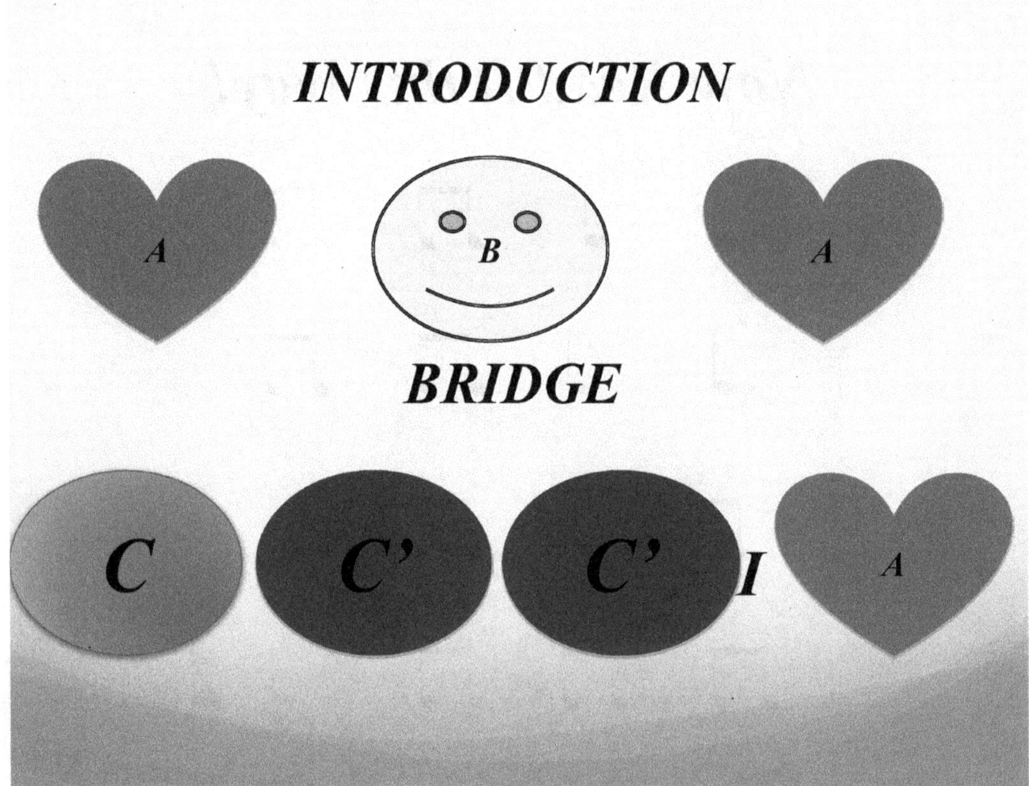

FIGURE 8.4 Listening Experience 8, Slide 7

Introduction (1:57–2:02)
A (2:02–2:20)

(c) More Advanced Experience (Locomotor):

- Students will choose a partner, and then partners will choose another group of partners to be a group of four. These groups will form the basis of the locomotor movement to the piece.
- The teacher will show students the movements they will perform as they listen to the piece and move around the room (slides 8 and 9):
  For the A section: walk around the room and find partner at the end of the section
  For the B section: perform pat—clap—hands out—clap motion with partner
  (Students will use bridge music to find group of four.)
  For the C section: create a 4-beat circle movement as a group
  For the C' section: create a variation of the movement from C
- The teacher will give groups of four an opportunity to create their movements for C and C', and all groups will rehearse movements together before listening to the piece.
- Students will listen to "Radetsky March" as they perform locomotor movements. Slide 10 provides a visual of the entire form of the piece.

"IN THE HALL OF THE MOUNTAIN KING" FROM *PEER GYNT SUITE* 9

Musical Selection:

"In the Hall of the Mountain King" from *Peer Gynt Suite* No. 1, Op. 46 by Edvard Grieg (from *The 50 Greatest Pieces of Classical Music,* performed by David Parry and the London Philharmonic Orchestra, 2009, X5 Music Group)

Tonality:

D Minor

Meter:

Simple Duple (4/4)

Musical Concepts Experienced/Addressed:

1. Form
2. Rhythmic Reading (Quarter Note, Two Eighth Notes, Half Note)

Musical Skills/Behaviors:

1. Creating rhythmic patterns using text and rhythm syllables
2. Creating movements to perform with rhythmic speech patterns
3. Performing selected rhythmic patterns (reading from notation) both alone and with the musical selection
4. Responding to formal sections through movement

Age Level:

The nonlocomotor version of this experience is appropriate as a way to review simple rhythms in primary grades. The locomotor activities might be more appropriate a bit later (2nd–3rd grades).

Suggested Procedures:

- Students echo-speak 4-beat phrases after the teacher using the words "tiptoe," "now," and "freeze." The teacher will show students an icon for each word as they speak (slide 1).
- After echo speaking some phrases, the teacher will show students a visual showing patterns that use combinations of these words. Students will speak and read these patterns using the text (slide 2).
- The teacher will ask students to create movements to perform for each different word and read the phrases again (slide 3) while also moving (first in a nonlocomotor way, then in a locomotor way).

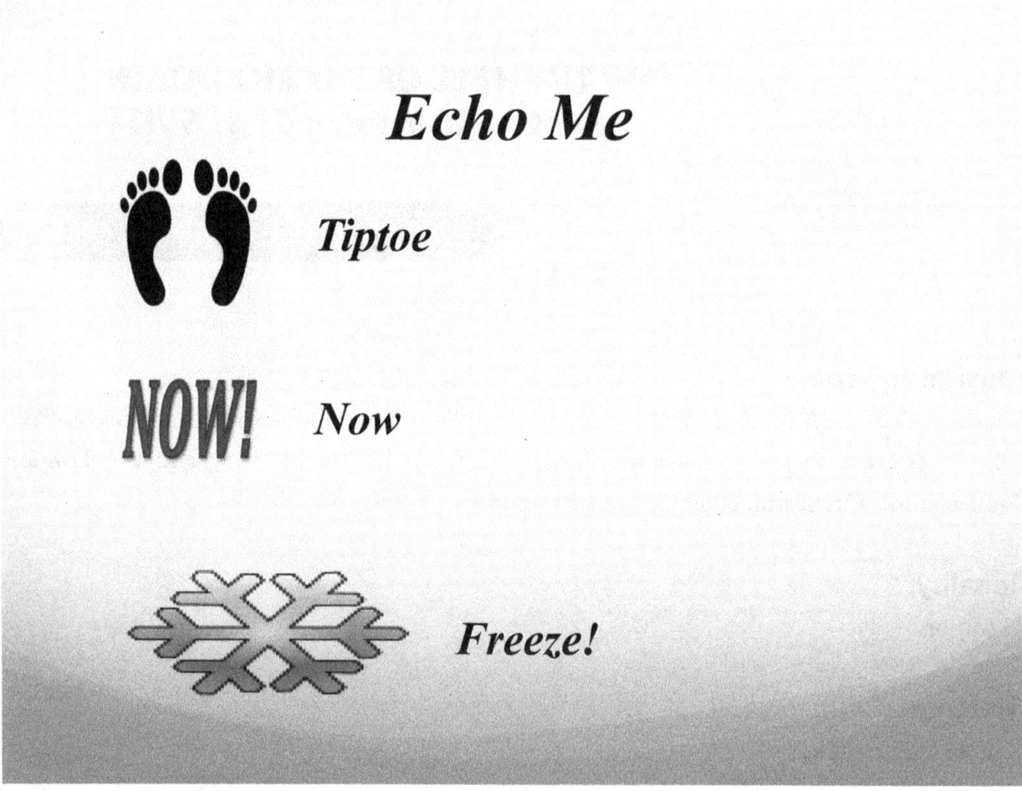

FIGURE 9.1 Listening Experience 9, Slide 1

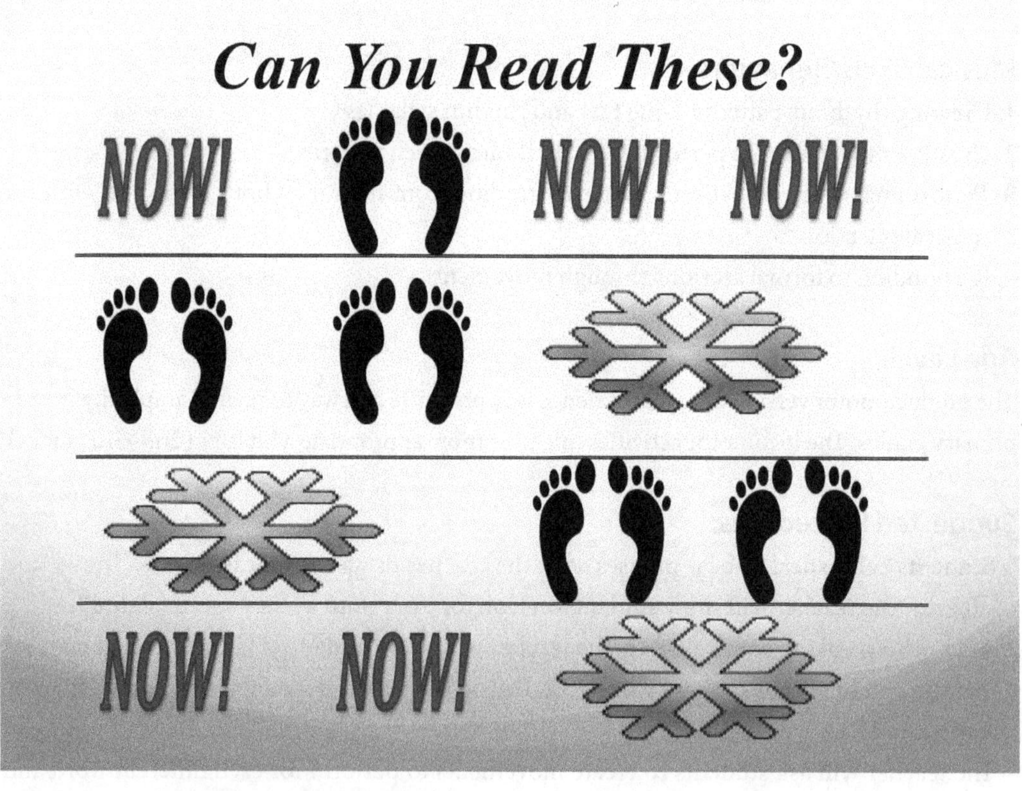

FIGURE 9.2 Listening Experience 9, Slide 2

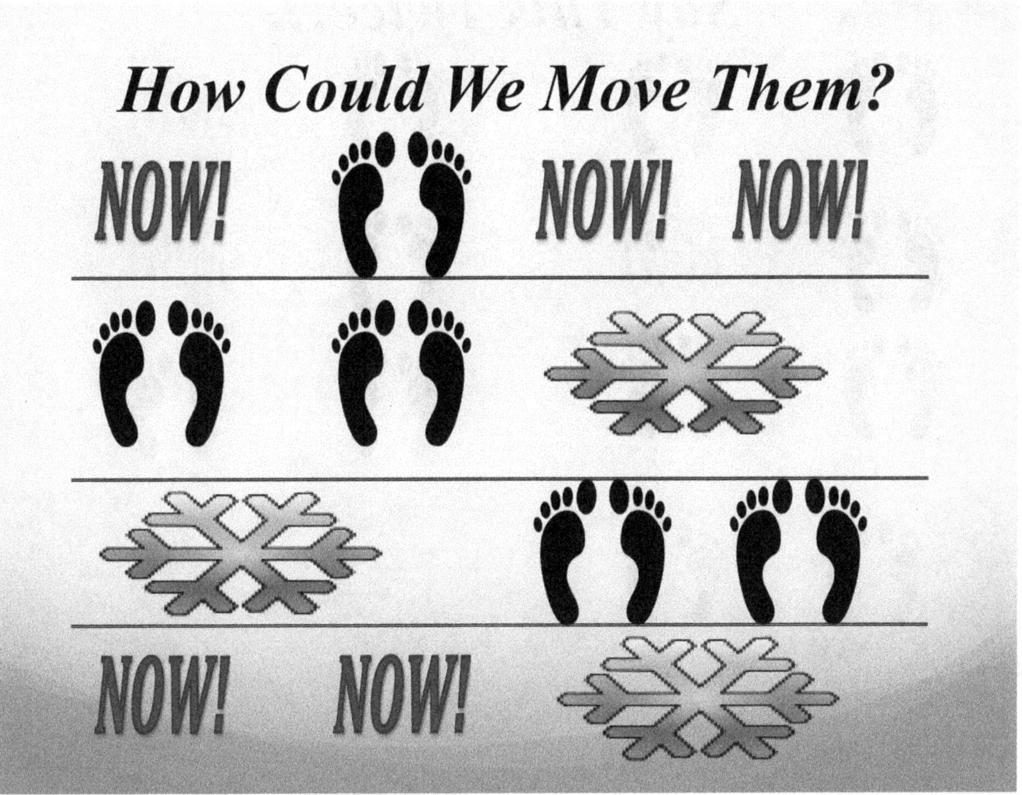

FIGURE 9.3 Listening Experience 9 Slide 3

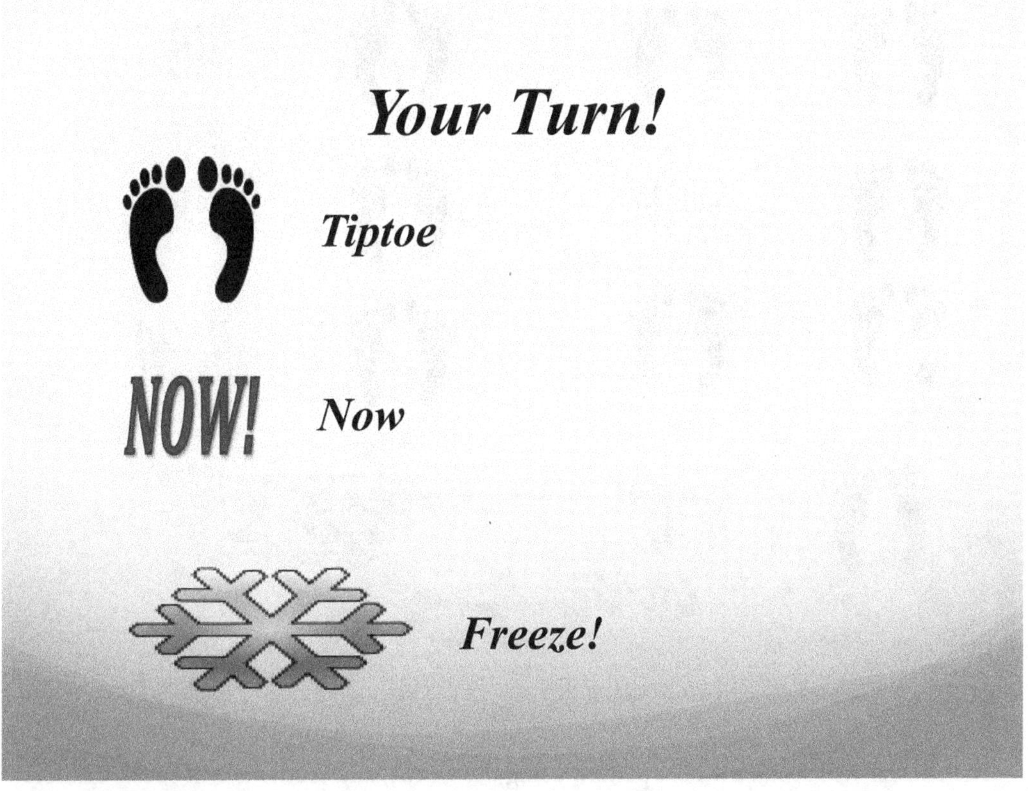

FIGURE 9.4 Listening Experience 9, Slide 4

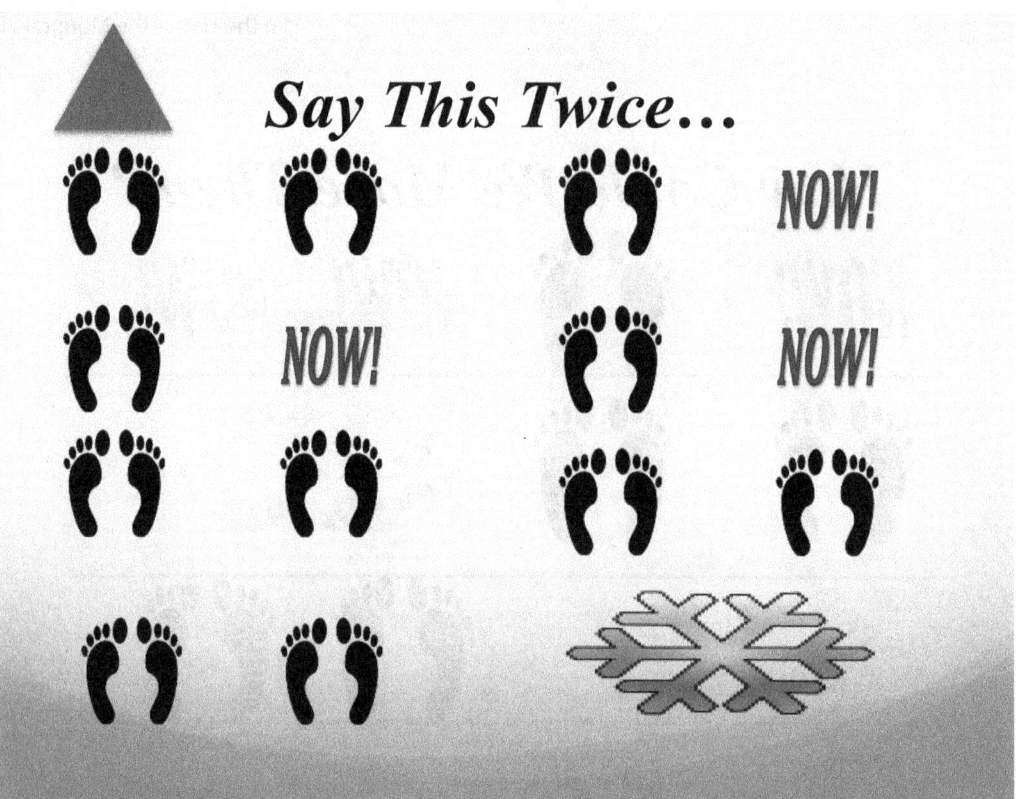

FIGURE 9.5 Listening Experience 9, Slide 5

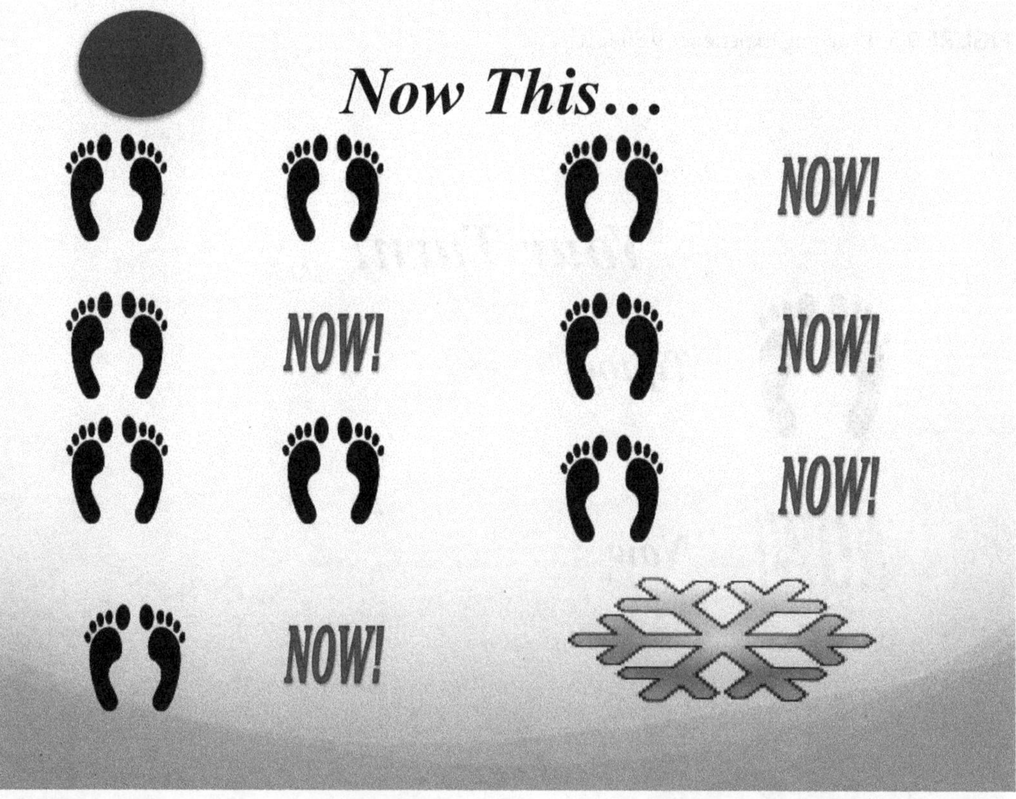

FIGURE 9.6 Listening Experience 9, Slide 6

– The teacher will speak a 4-beat pattern using the words, and students will speak a different 4-beat pattern (that they create) using the words (slide 4). After doing this a few times, the students will add their movements to the patterns they have created.

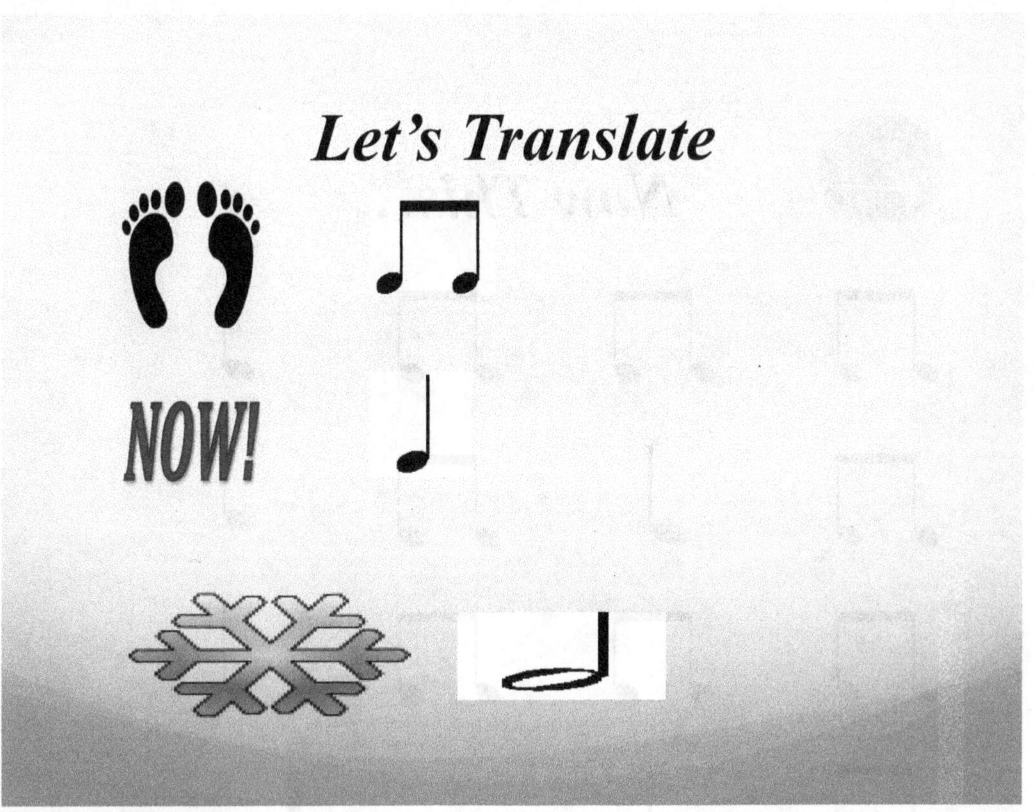

FIGURE 9.7 Listening Experience 9, Slide 7

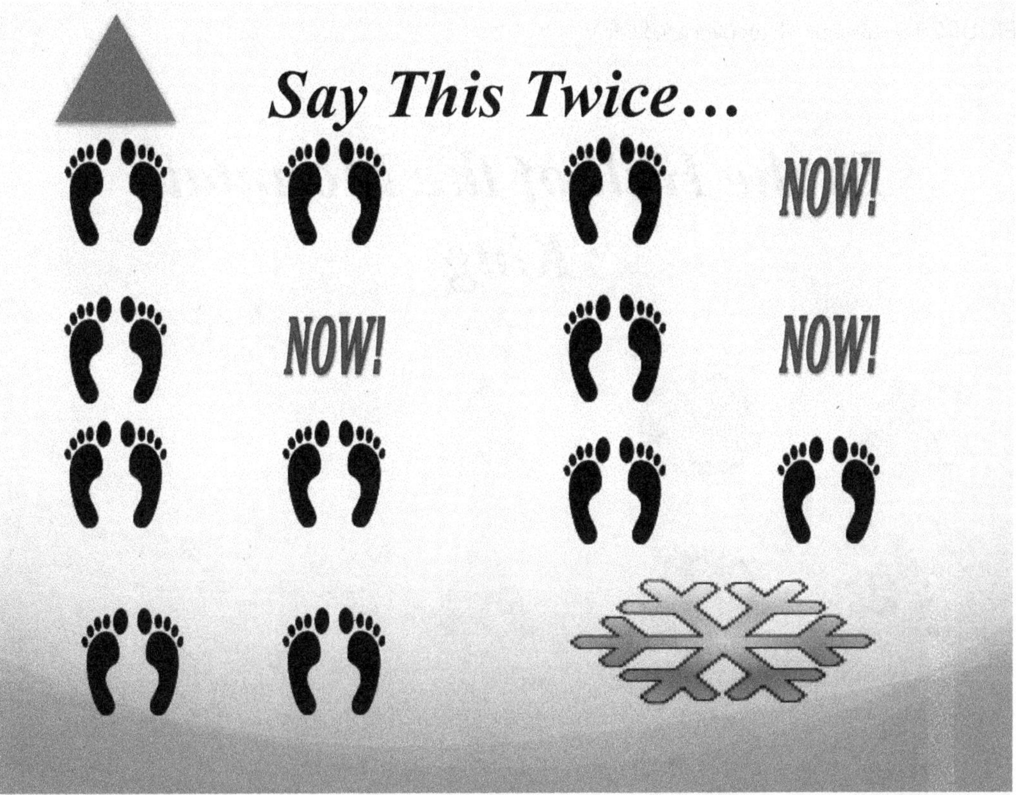

FIGURE 9.8 Listening Experience 9, Slide 8

– The teacher will have students look at a visual for the first section of "In the Hall of the Mountain King." Students will speak the pattern using the words. After speaking this pattern, students will repeat the activity using the visual for the second section of the piece (slides 5 and 6).

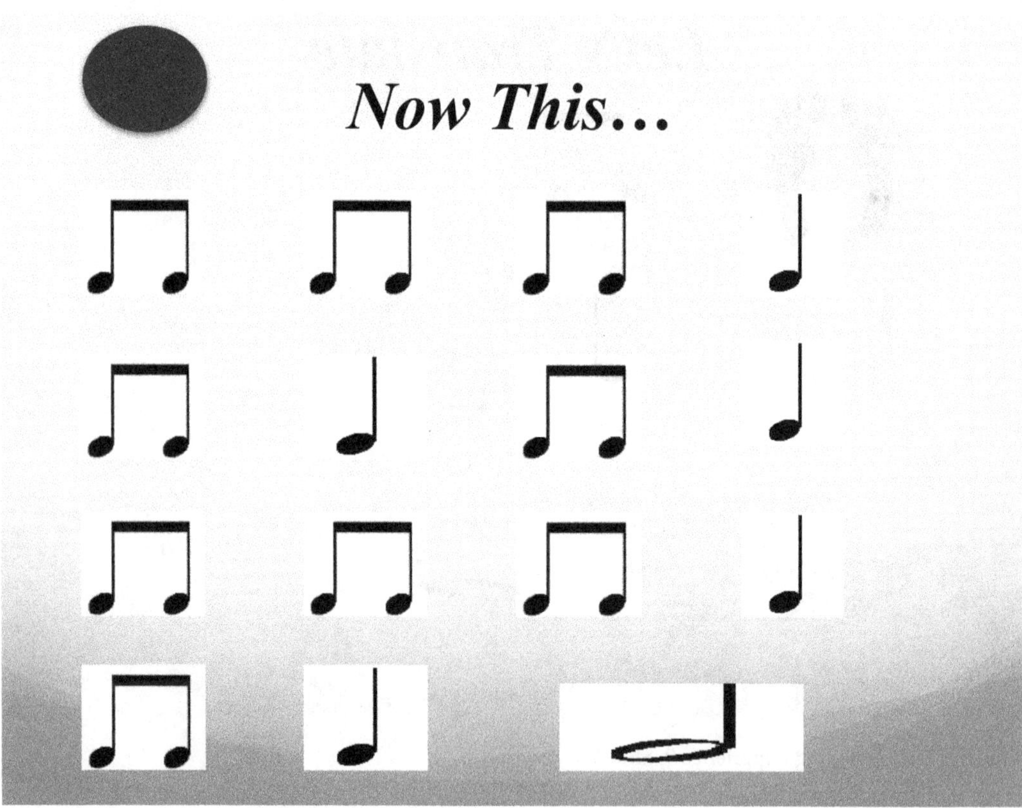

FIGURE 9.9 Listening Experience 9, Slide 9

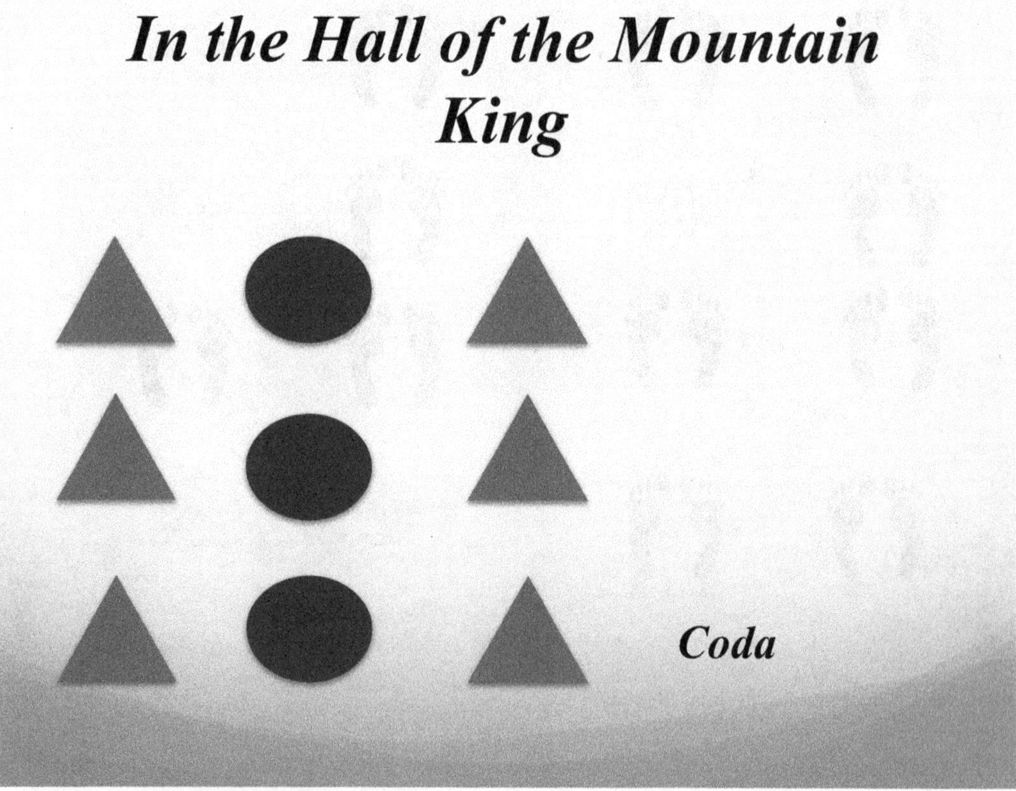

FIGURE 9.10 Listening Experience 9, Slide 10

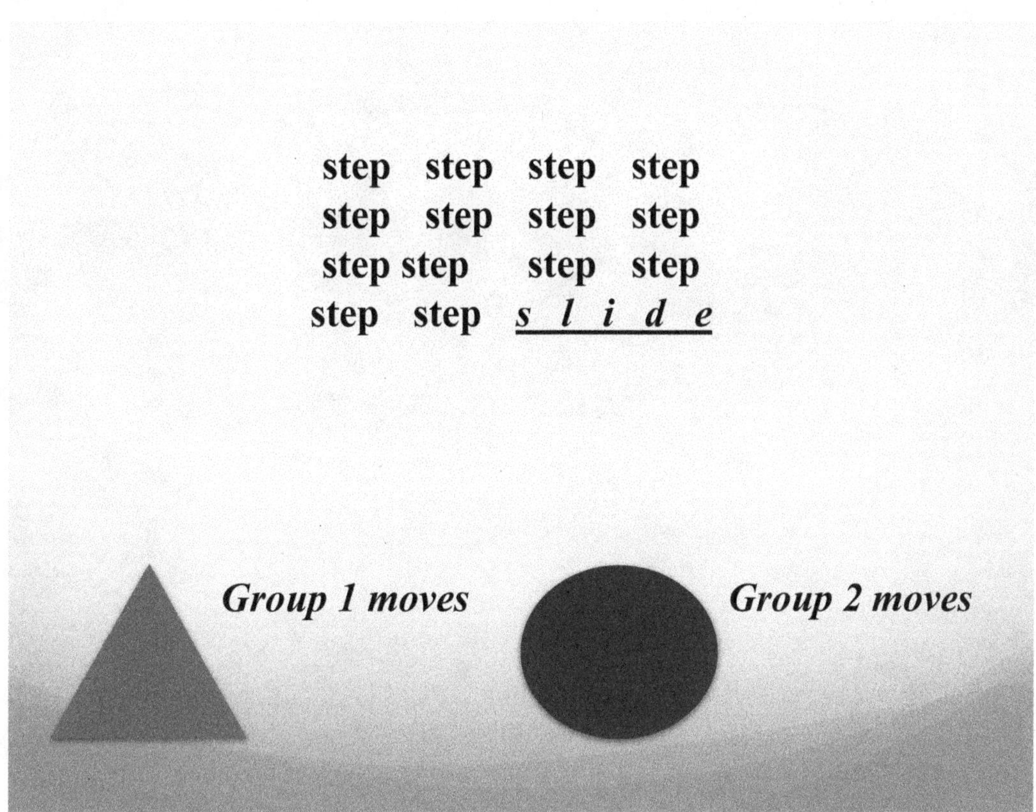

FIGURE 9.11 Listening Experience 9, Slide 11

- Students will translate the text into known rhythms and read the rhythm of each section using syllables (slides 7, 8, and 9).
- Students will view a visual of the form for "In the Hall of the Mountain King" (slide 10) and then listen as they tap the rhythm for the melodic line. The teacher can go back and use slides 8 and 9 if students need to view the rhythm for each section while they listen and tap
- Students will stand and move to the beat using the pattern found on slide 11. All movements are one beat long except for the "slide" at the end of the pattern which is 2 beats long.
- Students will divide into two groups. During the A section (red triangle), only group one will move, and during the B section (blue circle) only group two will move. Slide 12 provides a visual of the form students can view as they move.

10

"FINALE" FROM THE OVERTURE TO *WILLIAM TELL*

Musical Selection:

"Finale" from the Overture to *William Tell* by Gioachino Rossini (from *Drive Time-Autobahn,* performed by Barry Wordsworth and the London Symphony Orchestra, 2005, Sony Classical)

Tonality:

E Major

Meter:

Simple Duple (2/4)

Musical Concepts Experienced/Addressed:

1. Form
2. Melody/Harmonic Progression

Musical Skills/Behaviors:

1. Creating movements to accompany one formal section of the piece
2. Performing (singing) a melodic line corresponding to the harmonic progression of the formal sections of the piece
3. Responding to the formal section of the piece through movement

Age Level:

Singing the accompaniment to the formal sections of the piece along with the performance of locomotor movements corresponding to the form of the piece would make this more appropriate for intermediate grades (2nd–4th grades).

Suggested Procedures:

- Students will echo-sing 4-beat melodic patterns after the teacher using three pitches found on slide 1: do (green circle), la (purple circle), and sol (red circle).
- Students will view icons representing the harmonic melodies for sections A, B, and C of the "Finale," found on slides 2, 3, and 4. Each circle represents 2 full beats in the music. Students should sing each circle in the pattern as if it were a half note. Students should sing the pattern on slide 2 (A) twice, the pattern on slide 3 (B) twice, and the pattern on slide 4 (C) only once.

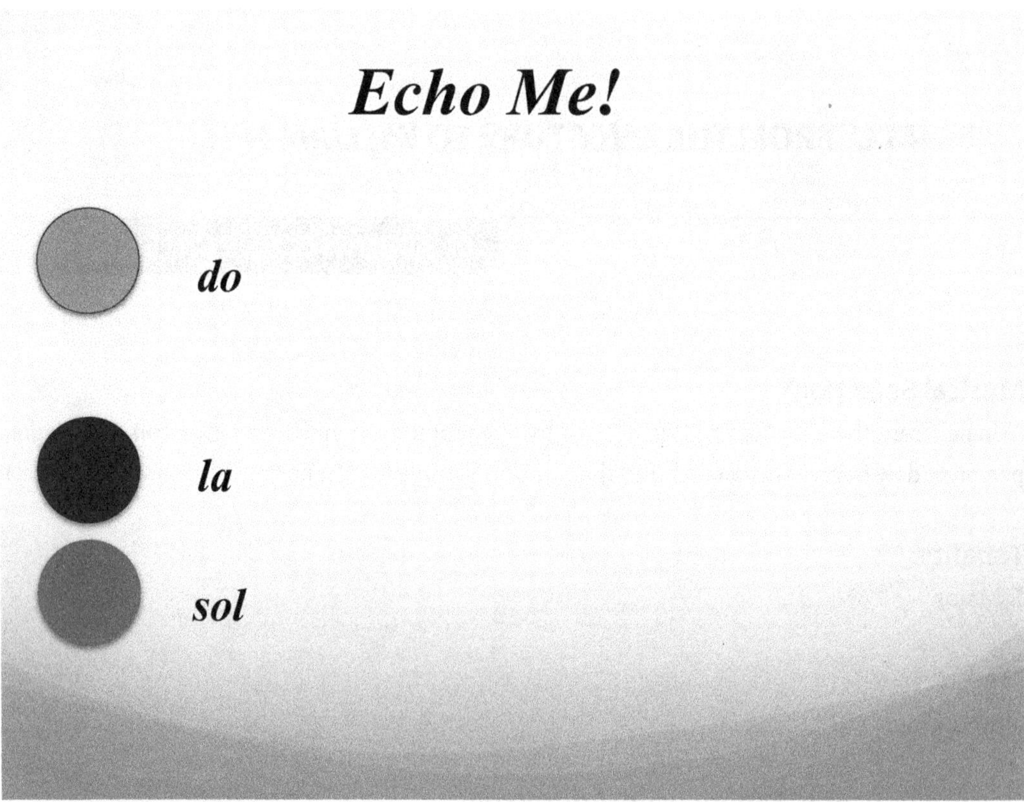

FIGURE 10.1 Listening Experience 10, Slide 1

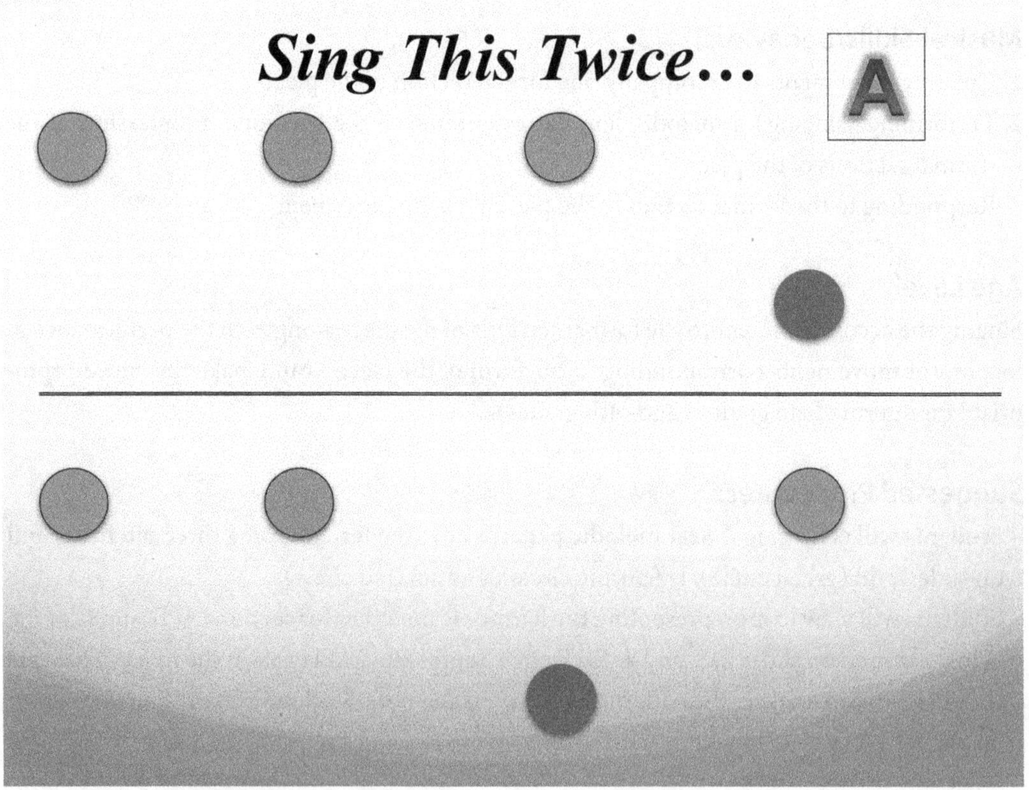

FIGURE 10.2 Listening Experience 10, Slide 2

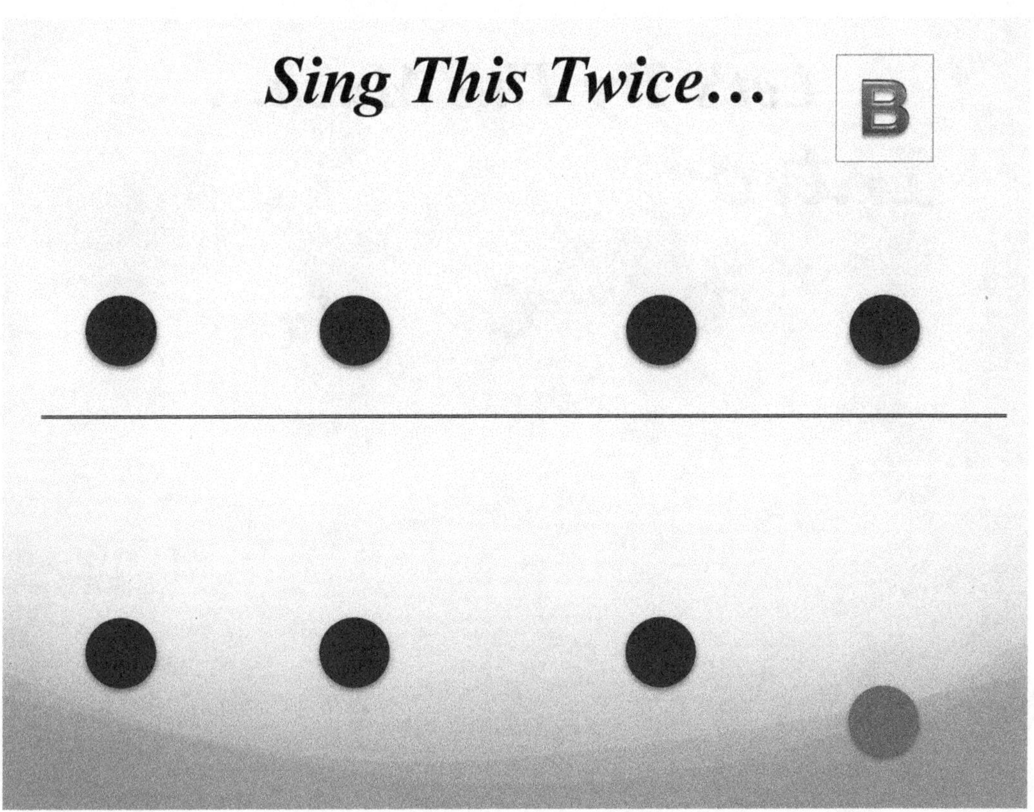

FIGURE 10.3 Listening Experience 10, Slide 3

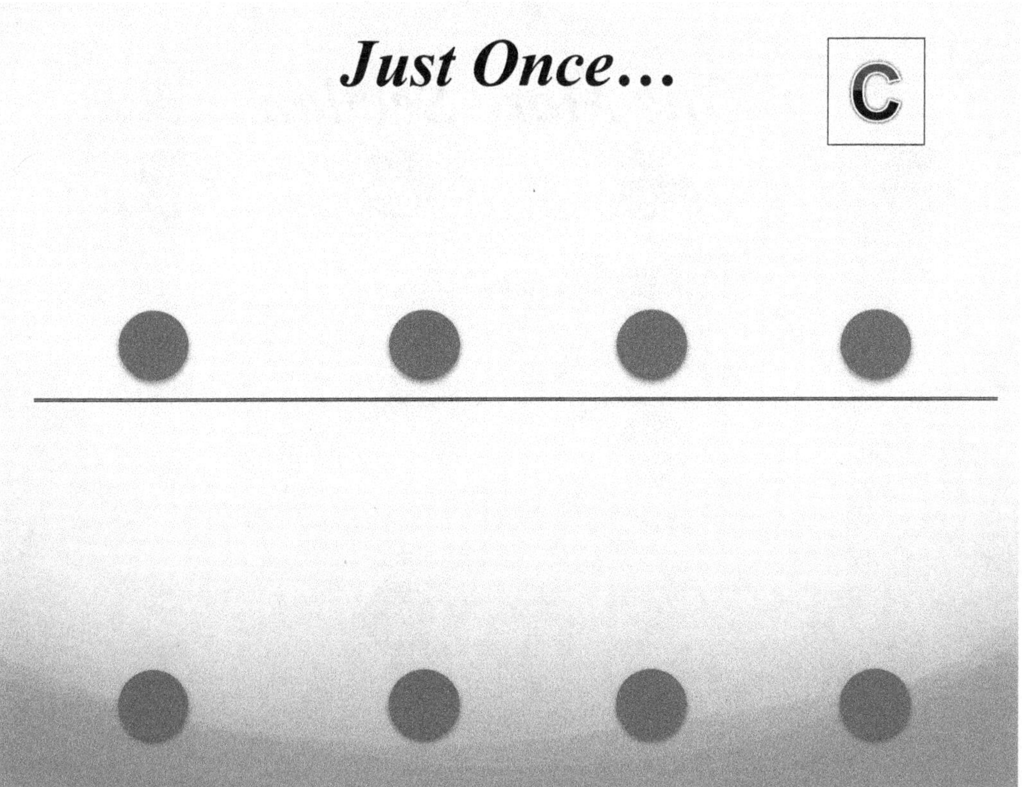

FIGURE 10.4 Listening Experience 10, Slide 4

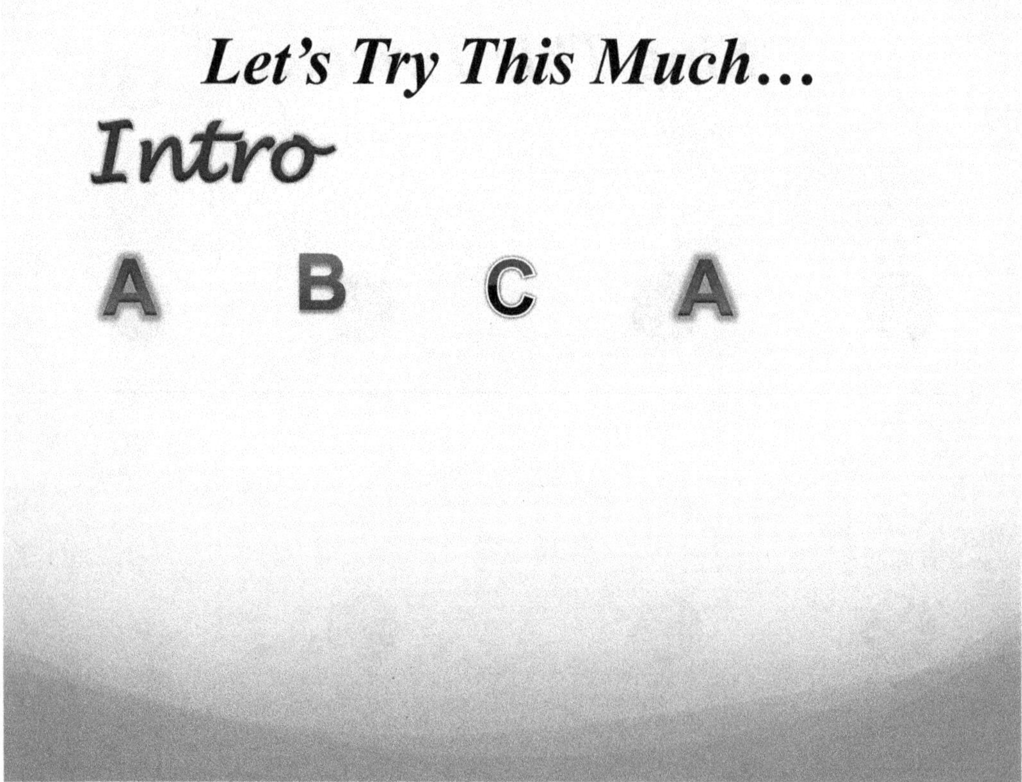

FIGURE 10.5 Listening Experience 10, Slide 5

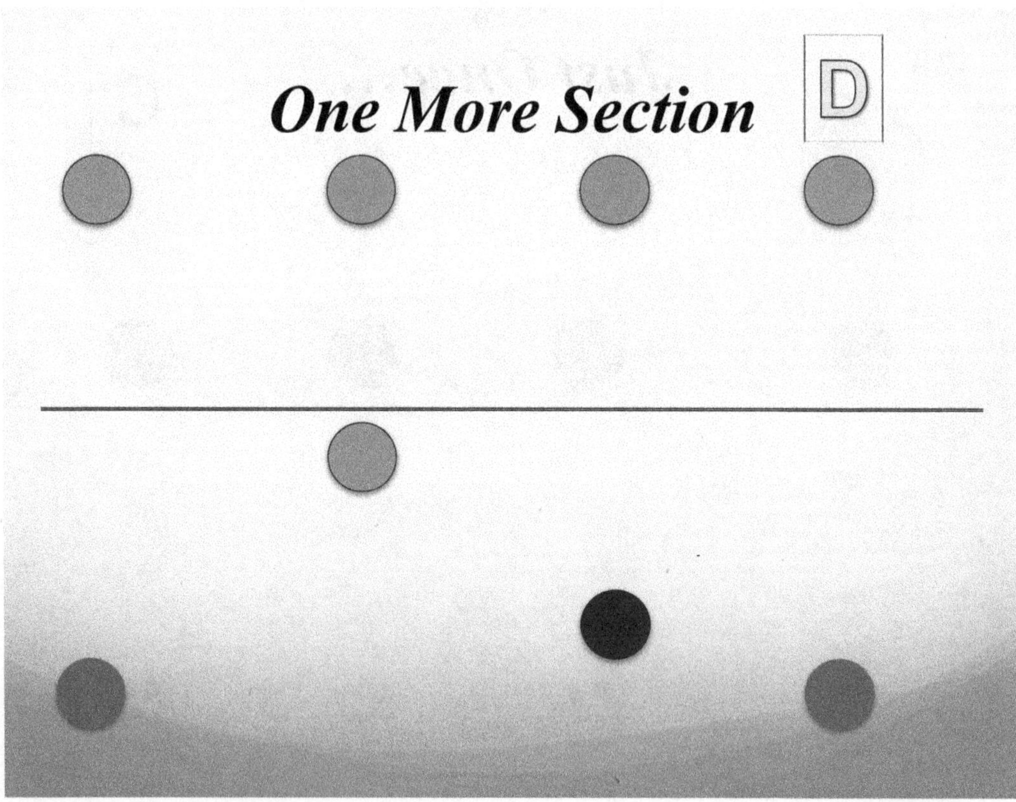

FIGURE 10.6 Listening Experience 10, Slide 10

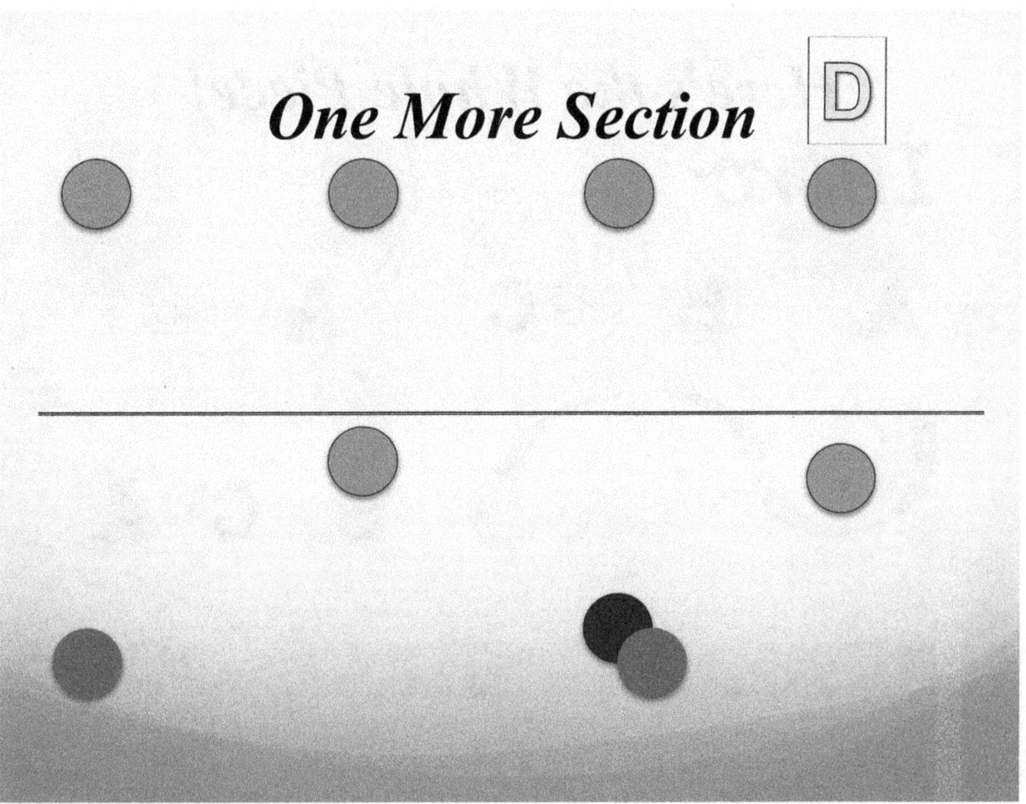

FIGURE 10.7 Listening Experience 10, Slide 11

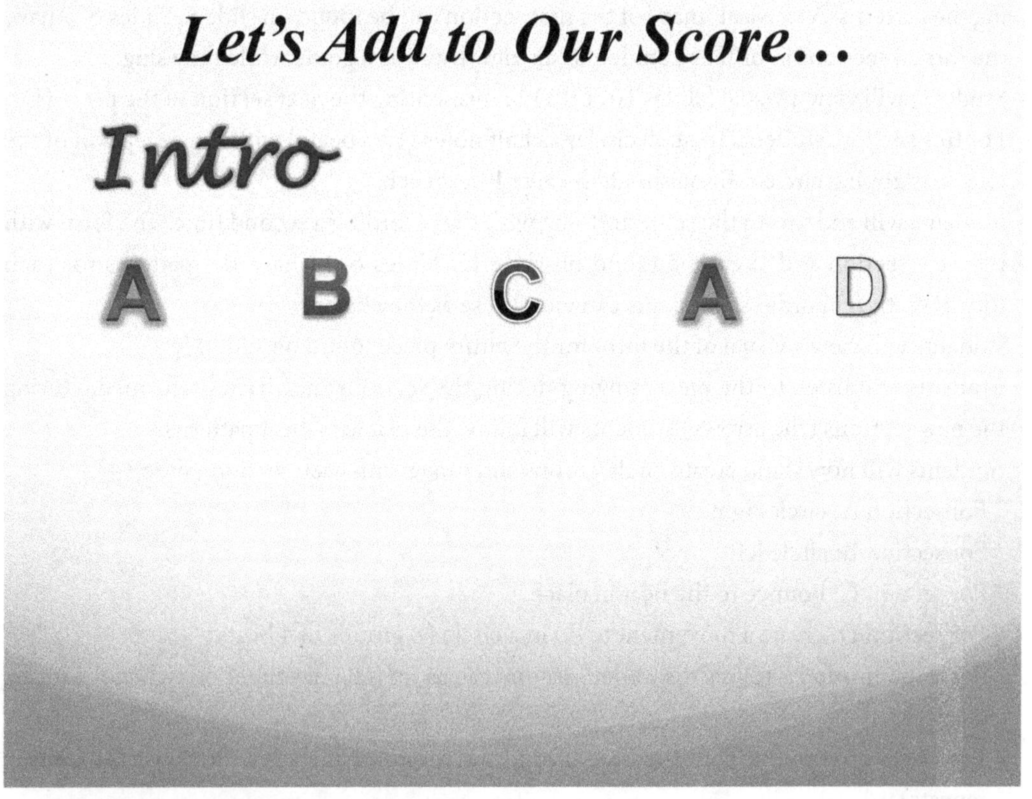

FIGURE 10.8 Listening Experience 10, Slide 12

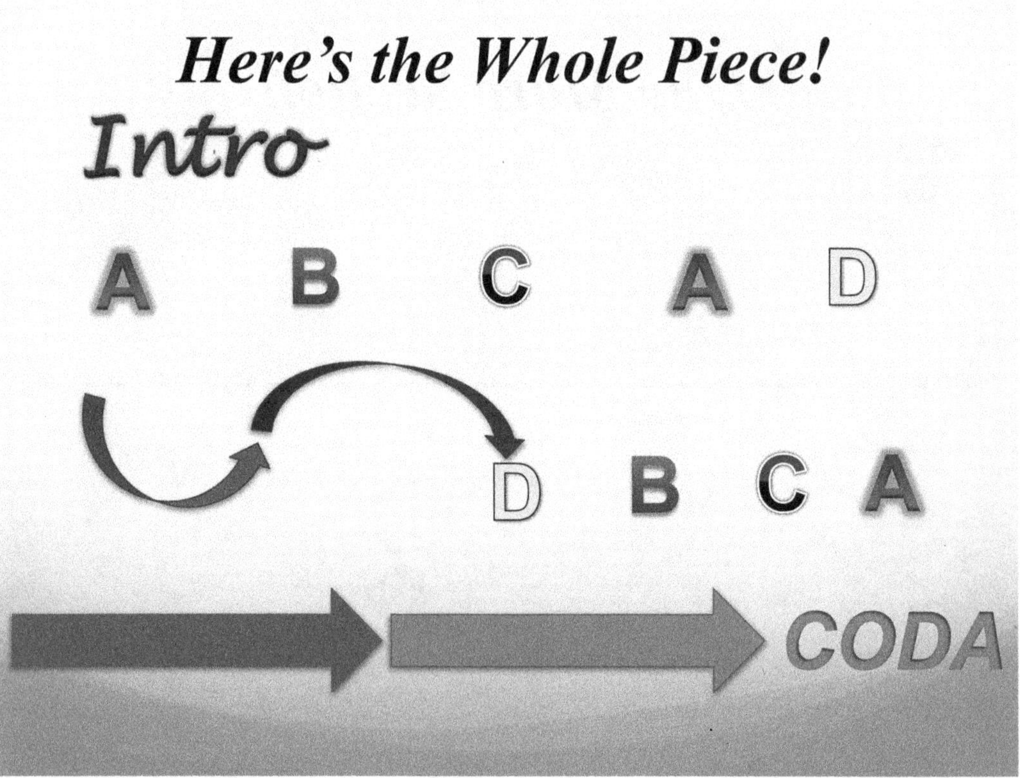

FIGURE 10.9 Listening Experience 10, Slide 13

- After singing, each of these students will listen to the first segment of the "Finale" while singing the patterns. A musical "map" of the first section can be found on slide 5. Slides 6–9 have the formal sections in order so students can view these as a guide while they sing.
- Students will view a visual (slides 10 and 11) representing the next section of the piece (D). For this section, students treat all circles as half notes (two beats) with the exception of the two overlapping circles. These should receive 1 beat each.
- Students will add this to the score and sing with the recording a second time. The form with the new section added can be found on slide 12. Slides 6–11 have the patterns for each formal section in order so students can view these as they listen.
- Students will view a visual of the form for the entire piece found on slide 13.
- Students will listen to the piece, singing during the sections they have performed. During the new sections (the arrows) students will follow the teachers' beat patterns.
- Students will now stand create circle groups and move with each section (slide 14).
  * For section A: circle right
  * For section B: circle left
  * For section C: bounce to the beat in place
  * For section D: create a movement to do in a circle (8 groups of 4 beats)
  * For arrow group 1: "follow the leader" around the room (change directions when the music changes)
  * For arrow group 2: walk to the beat around the room (change directions with the music repeats)

    * For the Coda: conduct
- The teacher may wish to have the entire class perform the circle dance as one group two or three times (making up a movement for section D that the entire class can perform) before dividing students into smaller groups and having them perform in small groups. Slide 15 provides a visual of the form for the entire piece.
- The timings for the piece are as follows:
    * Introduction: (0:00–0:12)
    * A (0:13–0:25)
    * B (0:26–0:37)
    * C (0:38–0:43)
    * A (0:44–0:56)
    * D (0:57–1:08)
    * Bridge One (first set of arrows) (1:09–1:30)
    * D (1:31–1:42)
    * B (1:43–1:54)
    * C (1:55–2:00)
    * A (2:01–2:12)
    * Bridge Two (second set of arrows) (2:13–2:47)
    * Coda (2:48–3:11)

"MENUETTO" FROM SYMPHONY NO. 35 IN D MAJOR 11

LISTENING EXPERIENCE 11

Musical Selection:

"Menuetto" from Symphony No. 35 (Haffner) in D Major by Wolfgang Amadeus Mozart (performed by The Chamber Orchestra of Philadelphia, 2014, Chamber Orchestra of Philadelphia)

Tonality:

D Major

Meter:

Simple Triple (3/4)

Musical Concepts Experienced/Addressed:

1. Form
2. Simple Triple Meter
3. Melody/Harmonic Progression

Musical Skills/Behaviors:

1. Performing (singing) a melodic line corresponding to the harmonic progression of the first two formal sections of the piece
2. Performing beat-related movements in simple triple meter
3. Responding to form through movement

Age Level:

Moving in a slow triple meter is one of the more challenging aspects of this experience. Due to this, the singing of a harmonic line that accompanies the melody of the piece, and the movement in longways sets, this activity would be more appropriate for intermediate or upper elementary school students (3rd–5th grades) who have had experience moving to slower tempi, singing in parts, and working in groups.

Suggested Procedures:

(a) Initial Experience (Nonlocomotor):

- Students will echo the teacher singing melodic patterns on solfege (slide 1).
- Students will learn and perform the harmonic lines for sections A and B of "Menuetto" (slides 2 and 3).

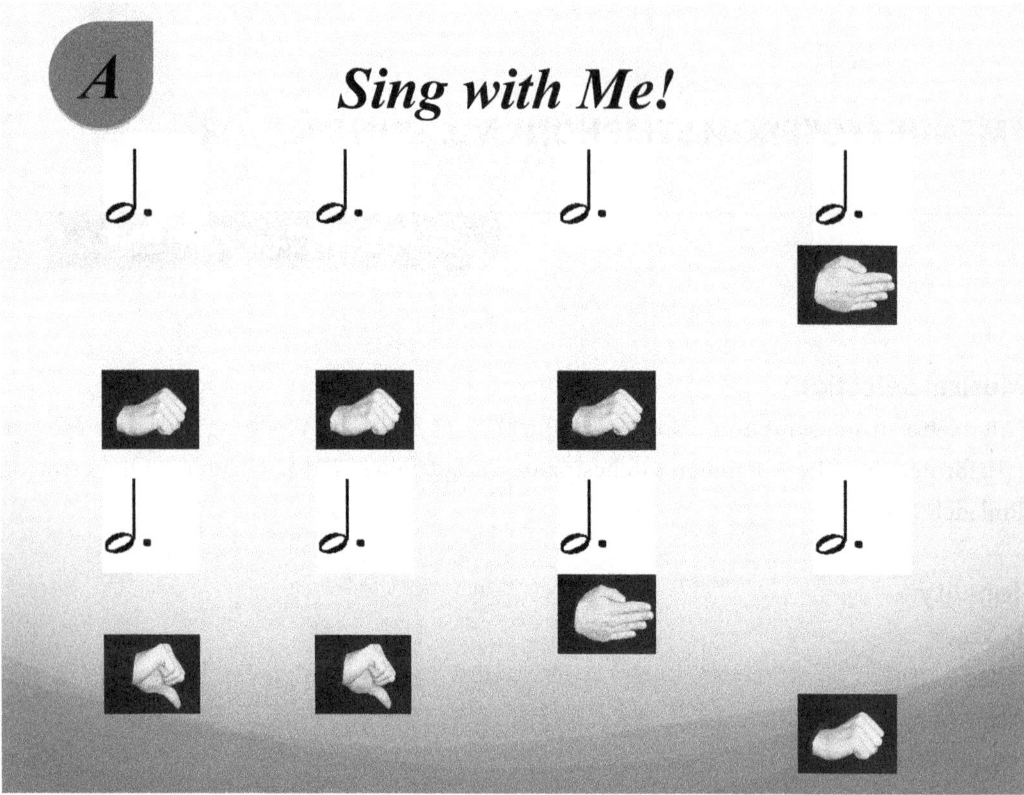

FIGURE 11.1 Listening Experience 11, Slide 2

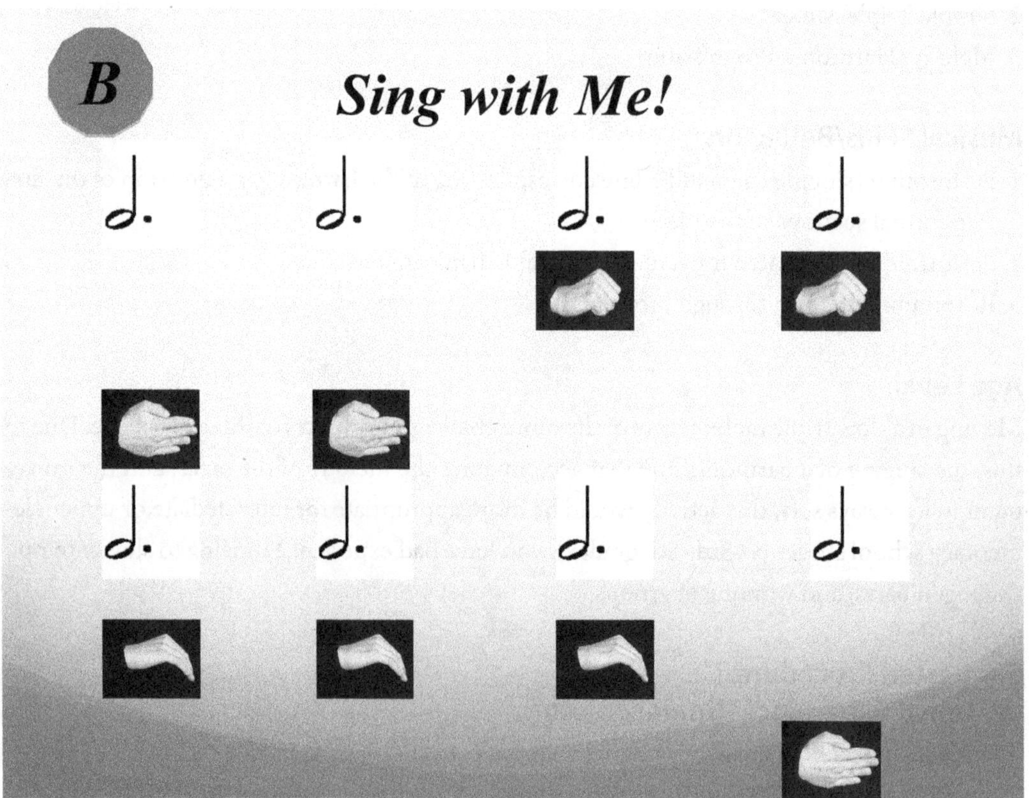

FIGURE 11.2 Listening Experience 11, Slide 3

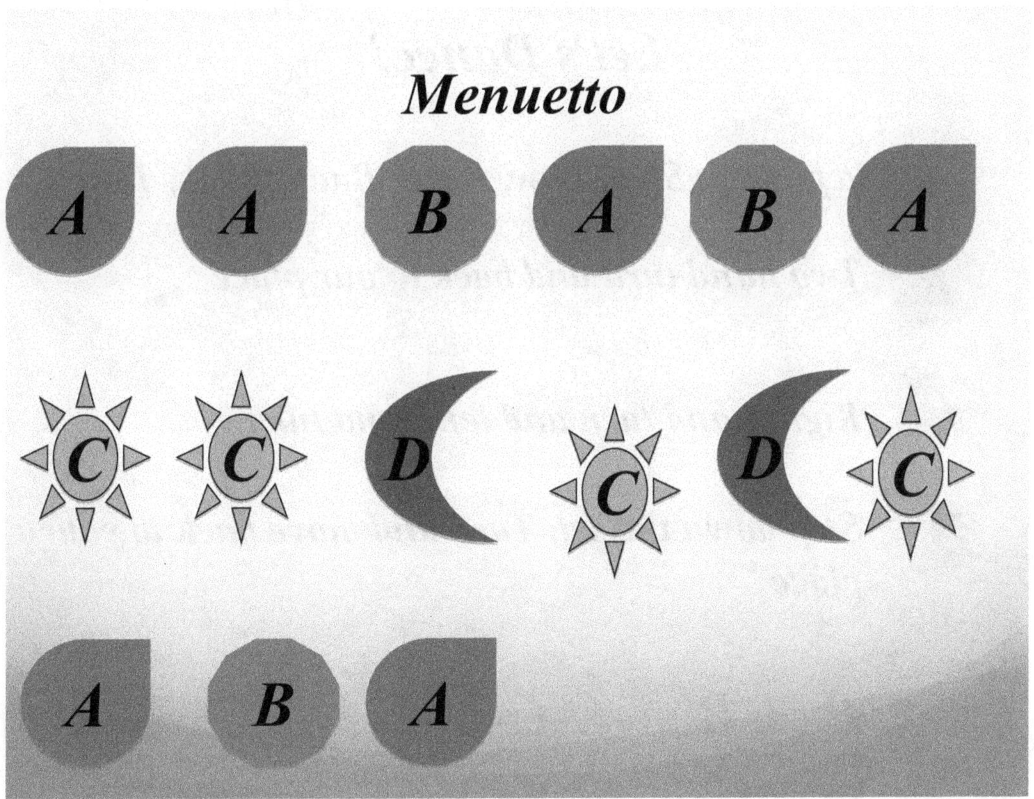

FIGURE 11.3 Listening Experience 11, Slide 5

- Students will view a map of the form of "Menuetto" (slide 5).
- Students will listen to the piece and do the following:

  For the A section: sing the harmonic line on solfege
  For the B section: sing the harmonic line on solfege
  For the C section: pat-clap-snap (8 groups of 3)
  For the D section: conduct (11 groups of 3)
  (The directions for the movements during sections C and D can be located on slide 4.)

(b) Formal Sections and Timings:

A (0:00–0:10)
A (0:10–0:20)
B (0:20–0:30)
A (0:30–0:41)
B (0:41–0:51)
A (0:51–1:02)
C (1:02–1:12)
C (1:12–1:22)
D (1:23–1:40)
C (1:40–1:50)
D (1:50–2:07)
C (2:07–2:18)
A (2:18–2:29)

Let's Dance!

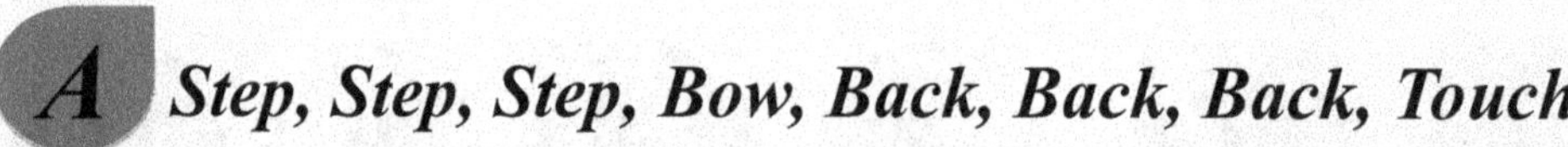

A
Step, Step, Step, Bow, Back, Back, Back, Touch

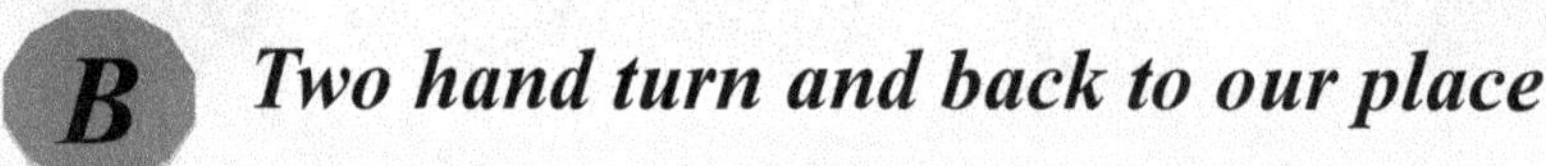

B
Two hand turn and back to our place

Right hand turn and left hand turn

Step down the set, Turn and move back to your place

A-A-B-A-B-A-C-C-D-C-D-C-A-B-A

FIGURE 11.4 Listening Experience 11, Slide 6

B (2:29–2:39)
A (2:40–2:50)

(c) More Advanced Experience (Locomotor):

- Students will find partners and form a longways set (partners facing each other in two lines). Students will view the visual for the dance while learning the locomotor movements for the listening experience (slide 6). It is suggested that students say the words from the on-screen directions (one per macro beat) as they are learning the movements.
  - For the A section: move toward partner for 3 macro beats and bow on beat 4; move away for 4 macro beats
  - For the B section: two-hand turn with partner for 8 macro beats (all the way around)
  - For the C section: 4 macro beat right hand turn (palms touching) and 4 macro beat left hand turn (palms touching)
  - For the D section: join right hands and move (as a set) one way for 4 macro beats; turn and join left hands and move the opposite way (as a set) for 7 macro beats
- Students will listen to the song again while performing a "Longways Set Minuet!"

"FIDDLE FADDLE" 12

LISTENING EXPERIENCE 12

Musical Selection:

"Fiddle Faddle" by Leroy Anderson (from *The Typewriter: Leroy Anderson Favorites*, performed by Leonard Slatkin and the St. Louis Symphony Orchestra, 1995, RCA Red Seal)

Tonality:

D Major

Meter:

The piece is notated in Cut Time (2/2). The slides below are notated using simple rhythms without a meter signature so that it can be used at a variety of age levels (feeling the quarter note as the beat).

Musical Concepts Experienced/Addressed:

1. Form
2. Melody/Harmonic Progression

Musical Skills/Behaviors:

1. Creating locomotor movements to perform with one section of the piece
2. Performing (singing) a melodic line to accompany one section of the piece
3. Responding to the form through movement

Age Level:

This activity applies both singing a countermelody and rhythmic reading to formal sections of a piece. For the sake of example, the countermelody is performed on solfege, and students would need to be comfortable with solfege and hand signs in order to perform some of the suggested activities. As a result, it would be more appropriate for intermediate elementary students (3rd–5th grades).

Suggested Procedures:

- Students begin by echo-singing using the four pitches found in the counter melody (do, re, low la, low sol). If helpful, the teacher can refer to the hand sign chart found on slide 1 of the PowerPoint presentation.

– Students will learn and perform the counter melody for the A section following the teacher's hand signs and then using the visual (slides 2–3).

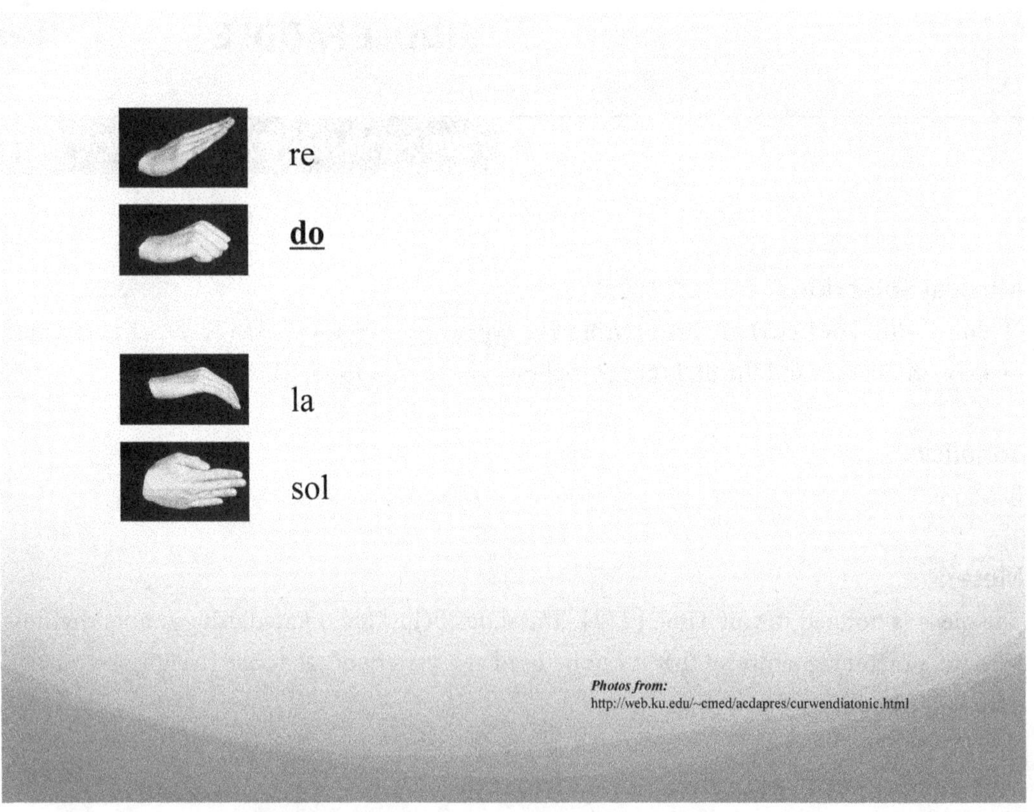

FIGURE 12.1 Listening Experience 12, Slide 1

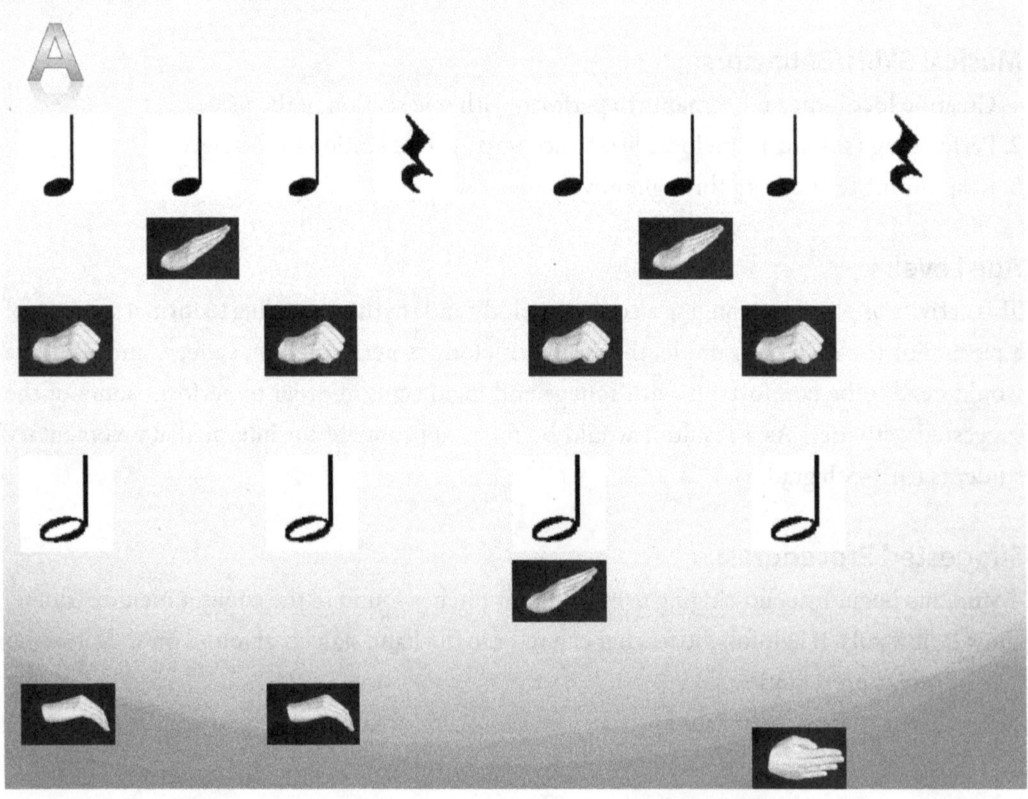

FIGURE 12.2 Listening Experience 12, Slide 2

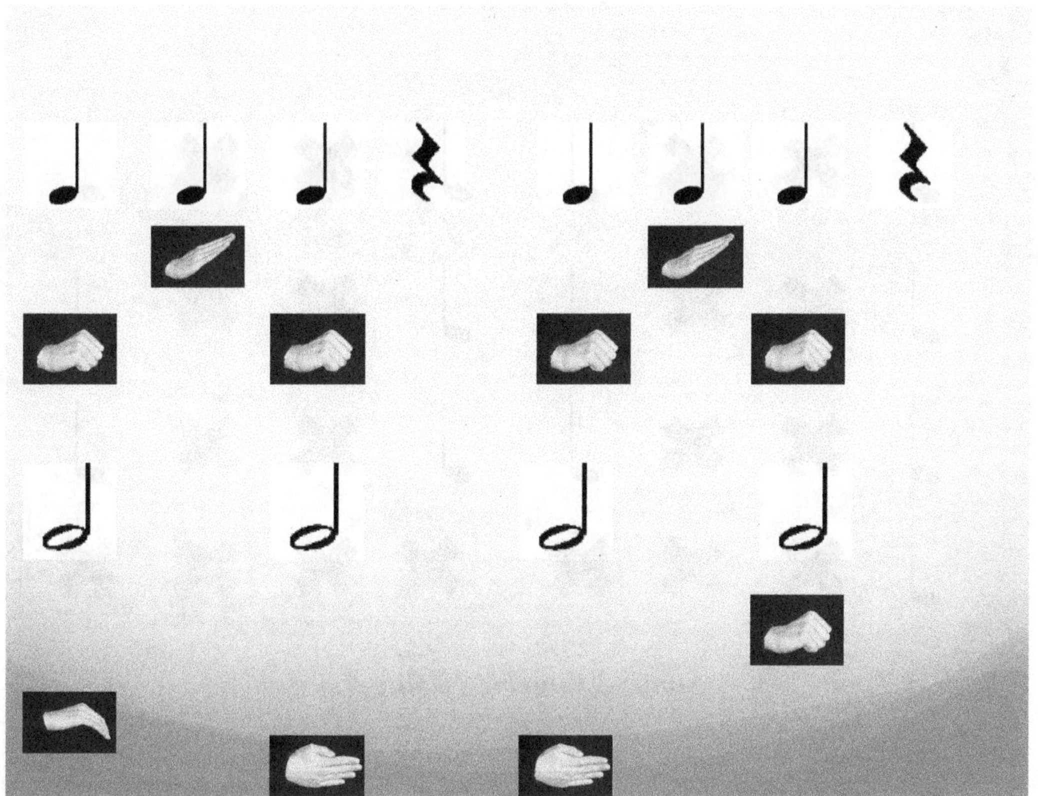

FIGURE 12.3 Listening Experience 12, Slide 3

- Students will listen to the first section of the piece (from 0:00 to 0:59). This segment corresponds with slides 2–8 and utilizes the following form:
  * A (slides 2–3)
  * A (slides 4–5)
  * B (slide 6)
  A' (slides 7– 8)
- Students should sing this version of the countermelody once before they sing with the recording so they are aware of how this repetition of the counter melody is different.
- As they listen, students sing the countermelody for A and keep a beat during the B section.
- Students will stand and find a place in the room. The teacher will return to the B section. Since the name "Fiddle Faddle" indicates silliness, the teacher will ask students to create a "silly" walk for the B section. Students will demonstrate their walks as the teacher plays the hand drum. Once students have experimented and decided upon their silly walk for B, they will listen to the first 59 seconds of the piece again, singing the countermelody for A and performing their silly walk for B.
- The teacher moves to section C and has students speak the rhythm (saying the syllables for the notes and snapping when they see an "x" on slide 9).
- Students will listen to section C (from approximately 1:00 to 2:22) and perform movements with this section (step in place and snap during first repetition; stepping in place and tapping with 2 fingers during the second repetition; stepping in place and tapping with 10 fingers during the third repetition).

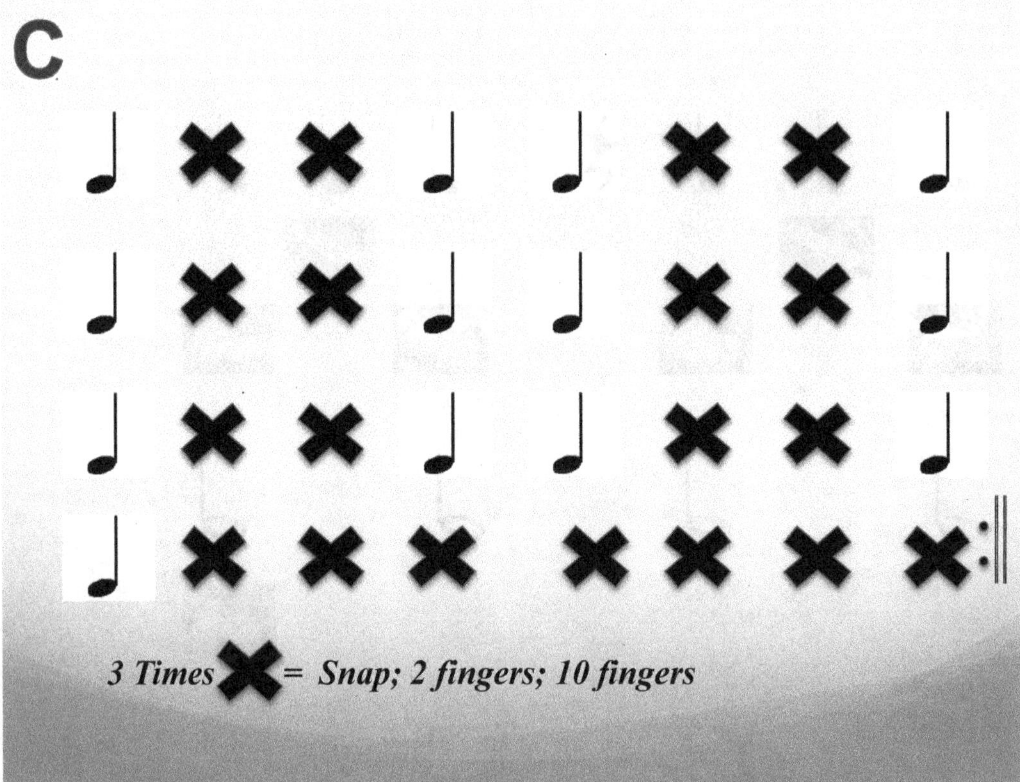

FIGURE 12.4 Listening Experience 12, Slide 9

– Students will listen to the entire piece, singing the countermelody on A, moving using their silly walks on B, and performing the step/snap exercise on C. The form for the entire piece is:
  * Introduction
  * A (slides 2–3)
  * A (slides 4–5)
  * B (slide 6)
  * A' (slides 7–8)
  Bridge
  * C (slide 9)
  * C (slide 9)
  * C (slide 9)
  Bridge
  * A (slides 10–1)
  * B (slide 12)
  * A' (slides 13–14)
  * CODA (slide 15)

13

"ENTRY OF THE GLADIATORS"

Musical Selection:
"Entry of the Gladiators" by Julius Fucik (from *40 Most Beautiful Classical Anthems*, performed by Vaclav Neumann and the Czech Philharmonic Orchestra, 2007, Warner Classics International)

Tonality:
The piece begins in C Major, eventually modulating to F Major for the final section.

Meter:
This piece is notated in Cut Time (2/2). Since the tempo makes it easy to read these rhythms as if it was in Simple Duple Meter (2/4 or 4/4), I have chosen to notate this using the quarter note as the beat. A teacher could easily convert this back to cut time if he or she wished for the students to experience this with the half note as the beat.

Musical Concepts Experienced/Addressed:
1. Rhythmic Reading and Improvisation (Quarter Note, Two Eighth Notes, Four Sixteenth Notes, Eighth Note–Two Sixteenth Notes)
2. Form
3. Simple Meter

Musical Skills/Behaviors:
1. Creating rhythmic patterns using both "circus words" and rhythm syllables
2. Performing selected rhythmic patterns (reading from notation)
3. Responding to form and meter through movement

Age Level:
Due to the rhythmic figures utilized in this piece, it would be more appropriate for intermediate or upper elementary students (4th–6th grades).

Suggested Procedures:
– The teacher begins by using four pictures associated with the circus (slide 1):
  a. Circus (two eighth notes)
  b. Clown (quarter note)

c. Unicycle (four sixteenth notes)

d. Heart representing the words "We love the ..."

(one eighth note followed by two sixteenth notes)

- The teacher speaks 4-beat patterns using combinations of the "circus" words, and students echo.
- The teacher shows combinations of the pictures (slide 2), and students speak the patterns in tempo using the "circus" words. The teacher will draw students' attention to the visual of the mouse on the final beat (indicating 1 beat of silence).
- The teacher will speak a 4-beat pattern using circus words, and the students will speak a 4-beat pattern using a different combination of the four words.
- Students will speak a pattern using "circus" words that corresponds with the A section of "Entry of the Gladiators" (slides 3 and 4 of the PowerPoint).
- Students will listen to the A section (0:00–0:42) and "tap" the rhythm with two fingertips (drumsticks) as they whisper the words.
- The teacher will show students a visual of the specific rhythmic figures that corresponds with each "circus" word (slide 5). Students will echo-speak and create using rhythm syllables instead of "circus" words.
- Students will look at a visual for the A section once again. This time, the visual will show rhythmic notation (slides 6–7). Students will speak on rhythm syllables and tap and then whisper and tap as they listen to the A section.
- Students will view a map of the rest of the piece. During the section B (slide 8) students will conduct in place. The B section occurs from approximately 0:43 to 1:15 and then repeats.

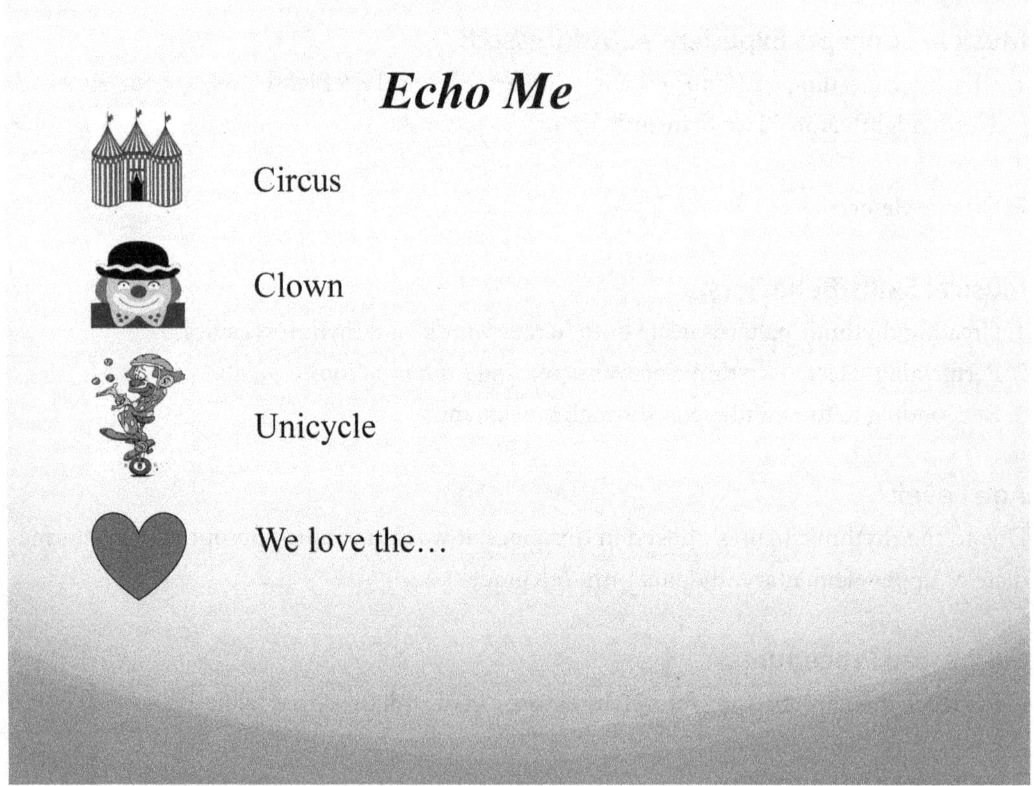

FIGURE 13.1 Listening Experience 13, Slide 1

FIGURE 13.2 Listening Experience 13, Slide 2

FIGURE 13.3 Listening Experience 13, Slide 3

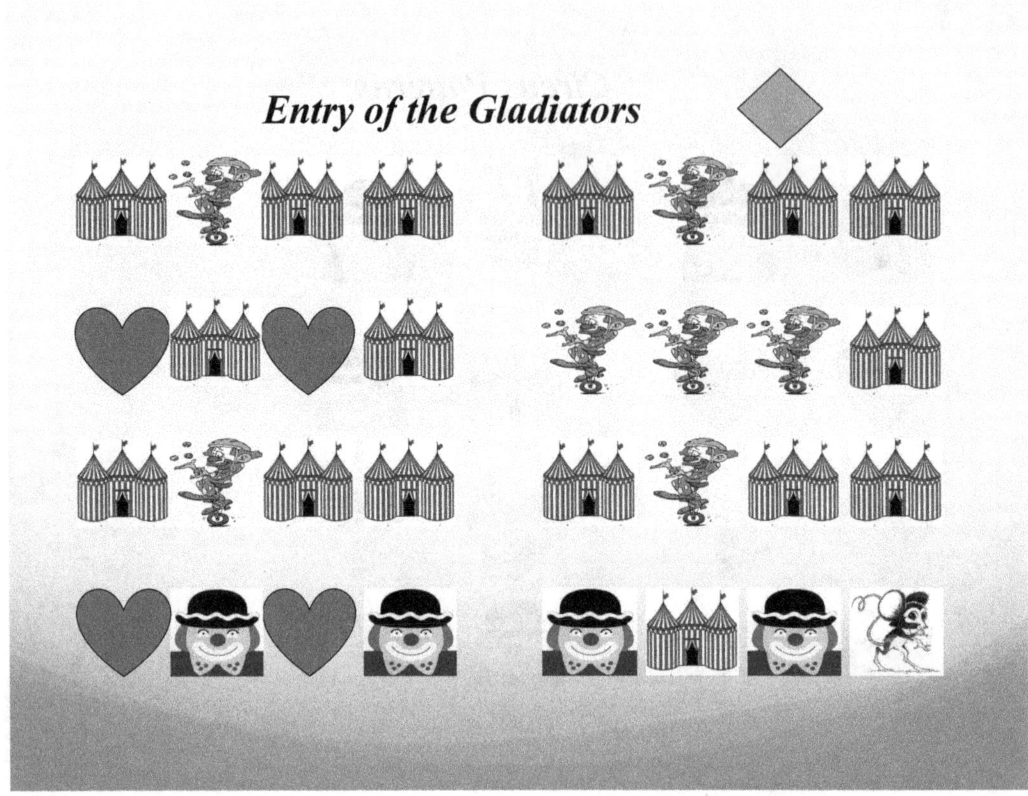

FIGURE 13.4 Listening Experience 13, Slide 4

FIGURE 13.5 Listening Experience 13, Slide 5

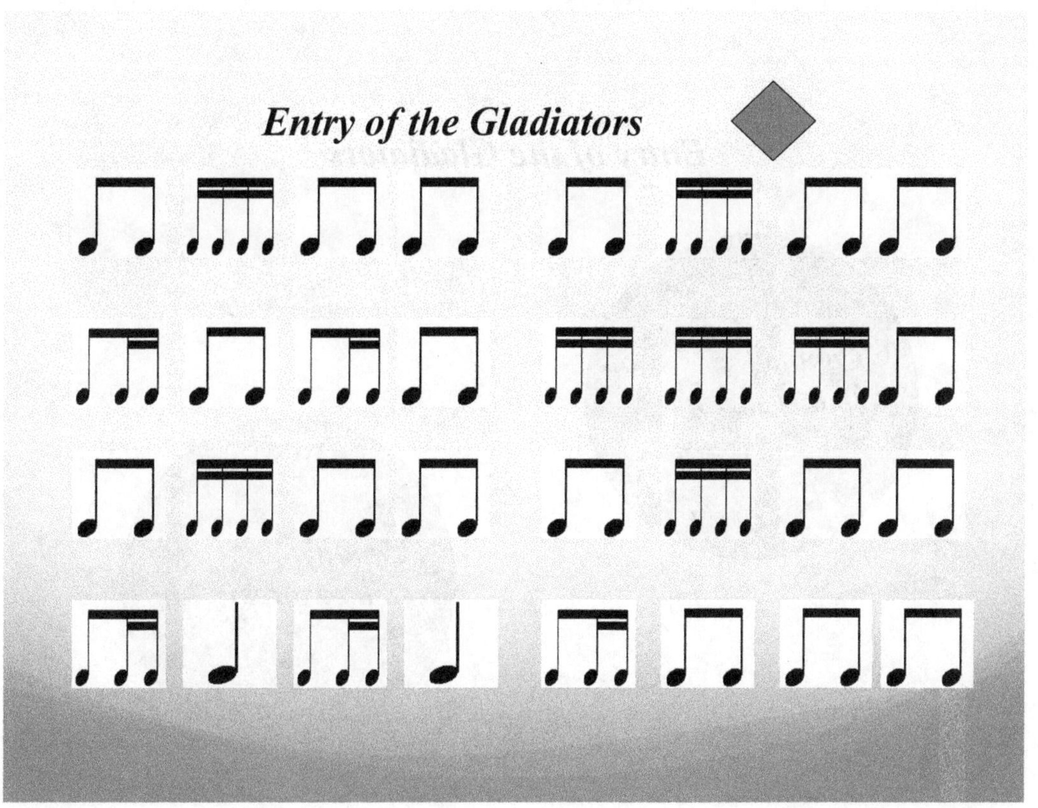

FIGURE 13.6 Listening Experience 13, Slide 6

FIGURE 13.7 Listening Experience 13, Slide 7

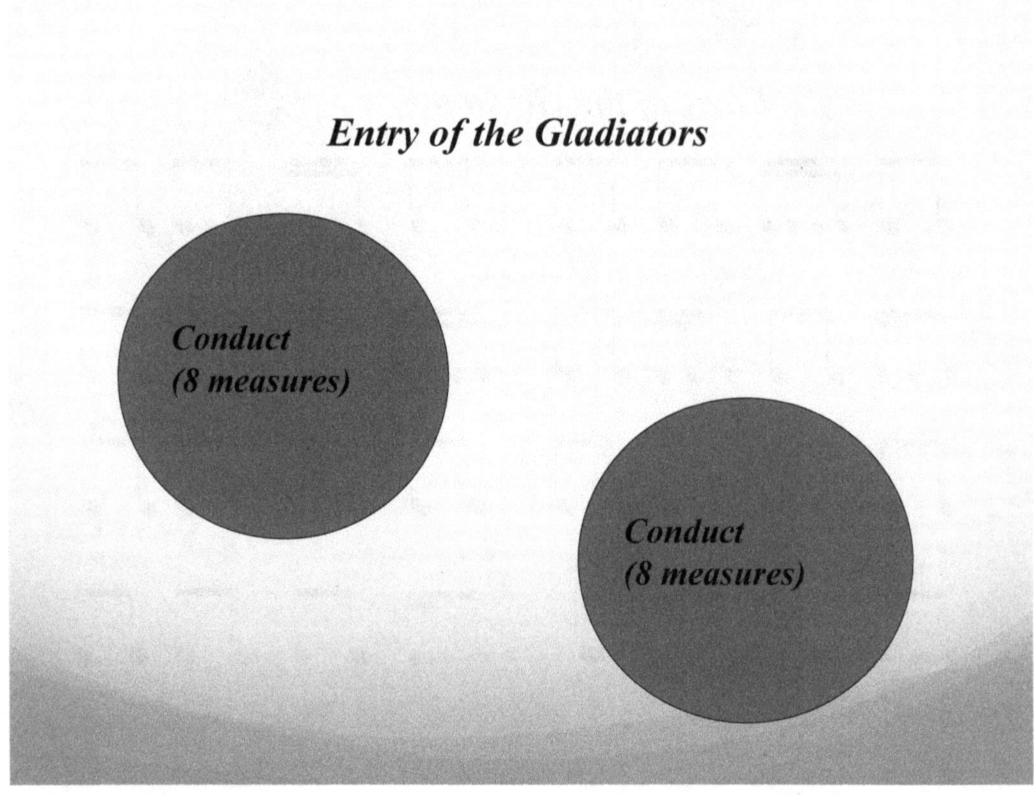

FIGURE 13.8 Listening Experience 13, Slide 8

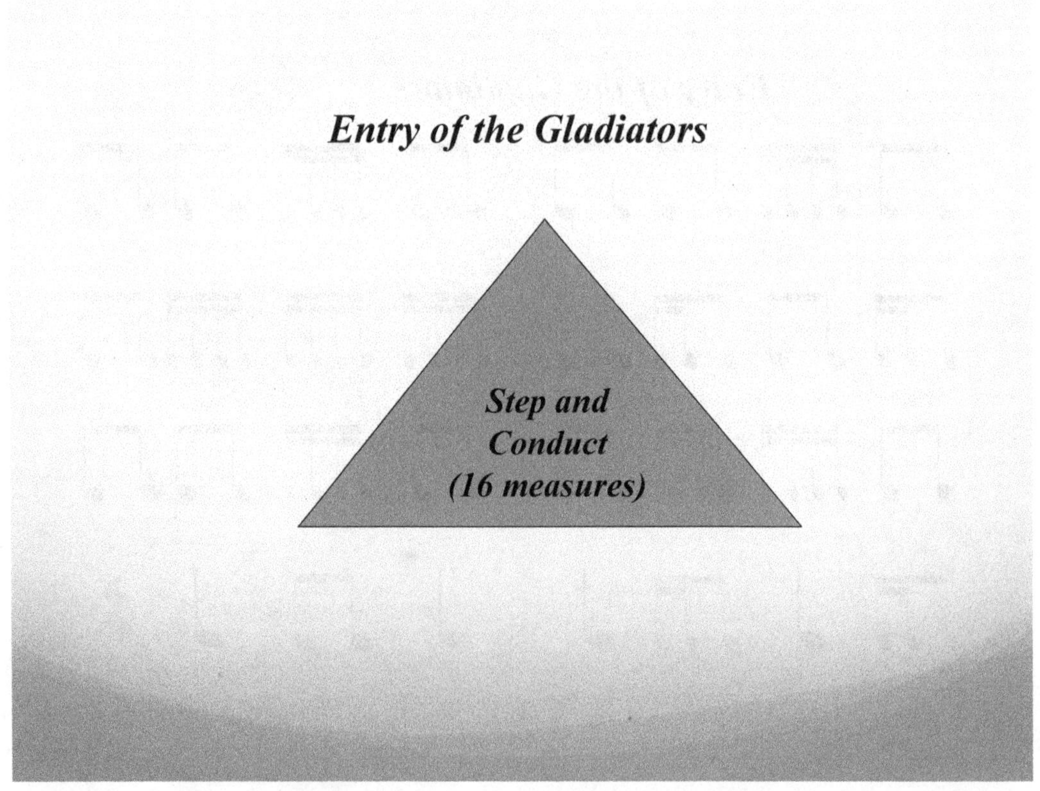

FIGURE 13.9 Listening Experience 13, Slide 10

- During section C (slides 10 and 12) students will march and conduct. Section C happens from 1:19 to 1:51 and repeats from 2:02 to 2:37.
- During the bridges between section B and the first repetition of C (slide 9) and between the first and second repetition of C (slide 11), students will march in place.
- The form of the piece is:
  * Introduction (0:00–0:12)
  * A (slides 6–7) (0:12–0:42)
  * B (slide 8) (0:43–1:15)
  * Bridge 1 (slide 9) (1:16–1:19)
  * C (slide 10) (1:19–)
  * Bridge 2 (slide 11) (1:52–2:02)
  * C (slide 12) (2:02–2:37)

14

"SCÈNE" FROM *SWAN LAKE SUITE*

LISTENING EXPERIENCE 14

Musical Selection:

"Scène" from *Swan Lake Suite* by Piotr Ilyich Tchaikovsky (from *The 50 Most Essential Pieces of Classical Music*, performed by Marko Munih and the Slovenian Radio Symphony Orchestra, 2008, X5 Music Group)

Tonality:

D Minor

Meter:

Simple Duple (4/4)

Musical Concepts Experienced/Addressed:

1. Rhythmic Reading (Quarter Note, Two Eighth Notes, Dotted Quarter Note–Eighth Note, Half Note)
2. Musical Phrases
3. Form

Musical Skills/Behaviors:

1. Creating movements to perform with musical phrases in the piece
2. Performing selected rhythmic patterns (reading from notation and moving) for specific phrases of the piece
3. Responding to the form through movement

Age Level:

The rhythmic material would make this more appropriate for upper elementary students (around 4th–6th grades).

Suggested Procedures:

- Students will listen to sections A and B of the piece. As they do, they will follow the teacher and "draw" each phrase while listening. The phrase structure is:

  A: Phrase 1 (0:00–0:14)

  Phrase 2 (0:15–0:27)

  B: Phrase 1 (0:28–0:39)

  Phrase 2 (0:40–0:55)

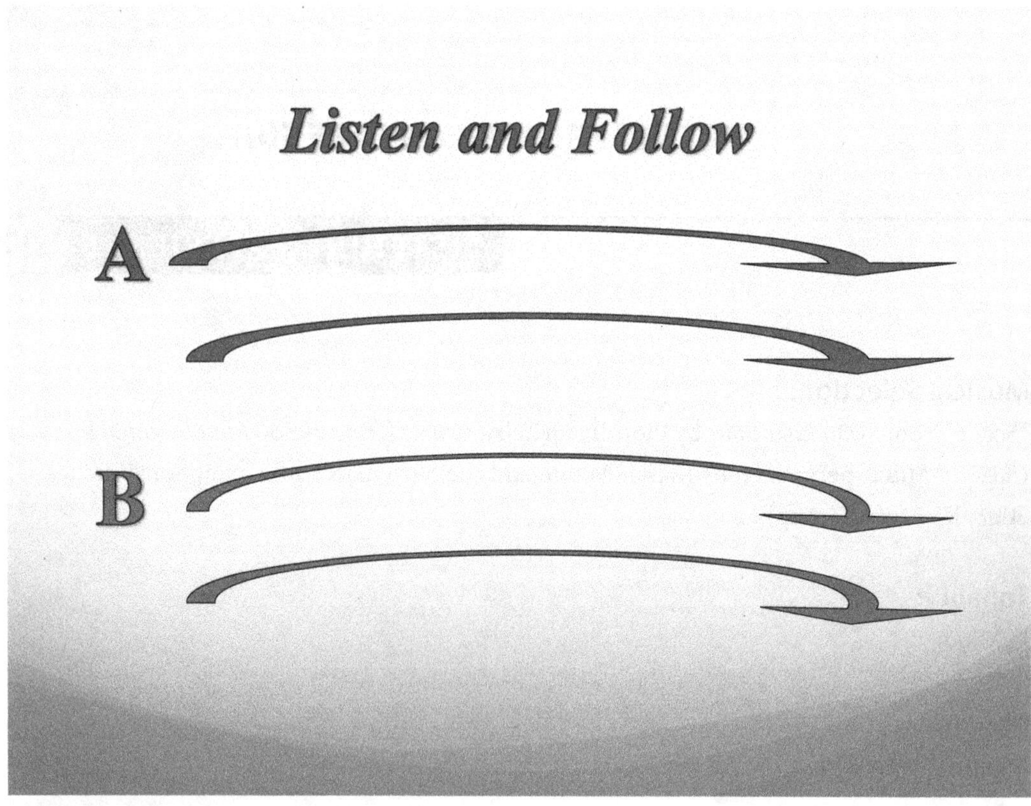

FIGURE 14.1 Listening Experience 14, Slide 1

- Students will view slide 1 and see a visual representation of the phrases for this section.
- Students will listen again but perform different phrase movements for A and B. Initially, the teacher might ask for suggestions that the class can perform as an entire group. After this, the teacher could have students in groups of two and have one student choose a way to move the phrase for A and another choose the way to move for B.
- After doing this, the teacher will show students slides 2 and 3. Student will echo speak rhythmic patterns using the rhythms found on slide 2 and then read the rhythm for slide 3.
- Students will then see another version of the rhythm for A that includes one tied note (slide 4). Students will speak and perform the rhythm for A and then add the rhythm for B (slide 5).
- Students will listen to the first part of the piece again (0:00–0:55) and tap the rhythm as they listen.
- The teacher will show a visual representing the form of the entire piece (slide 6).
- Before listening to the entire piece, students will look at slides 10 and 12 so that they can speak and read the rhythms for B' and A' and describe how they differ from the original sections.
- Students will listen to the entire piece and tap the rhythm for the A, B, B', and A' sections. During the bridge of the piece, students will follow the teacher in keeping some type of beat motion such as moving arms from side to side. Slides 7–12 provide the sections of the piece in the order they appear in the music.

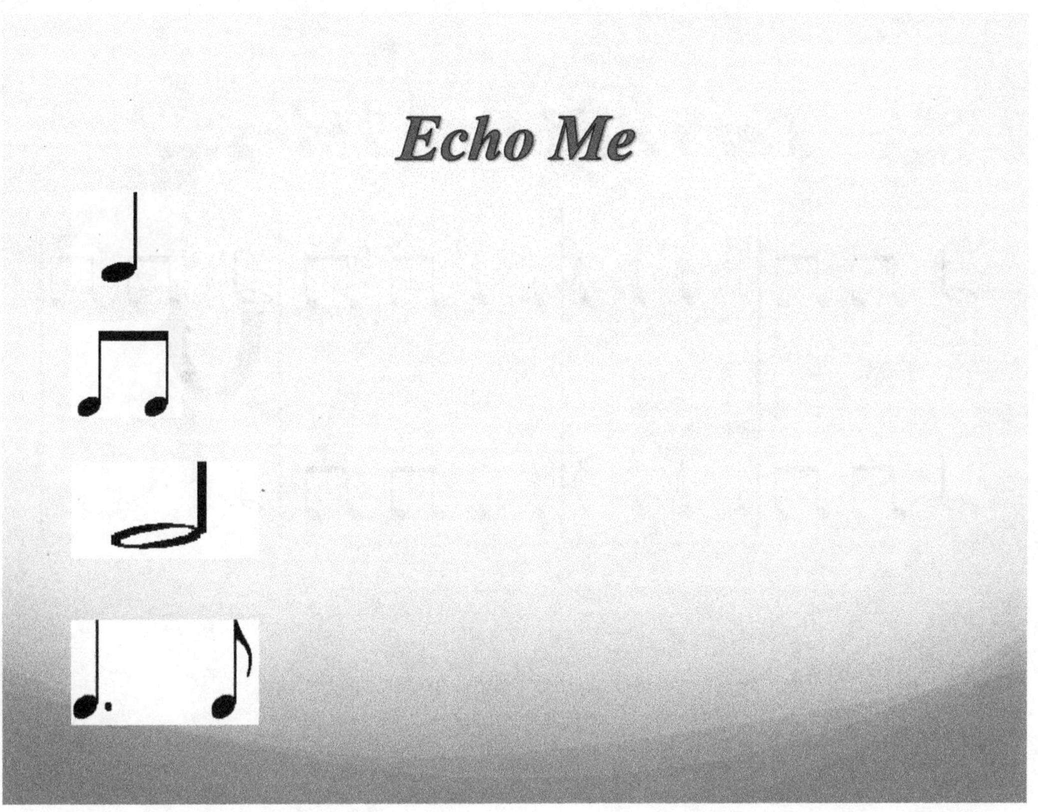

FIGURE 14.2 Listening Experience 14, Slide 2

FIGURE 14.3 Listening Experience 14, Slide 3

FIGURE 14.4 Listening Experience 14, Slide 4

FIGURE 14.5 Listening Experience 14, Slide 5

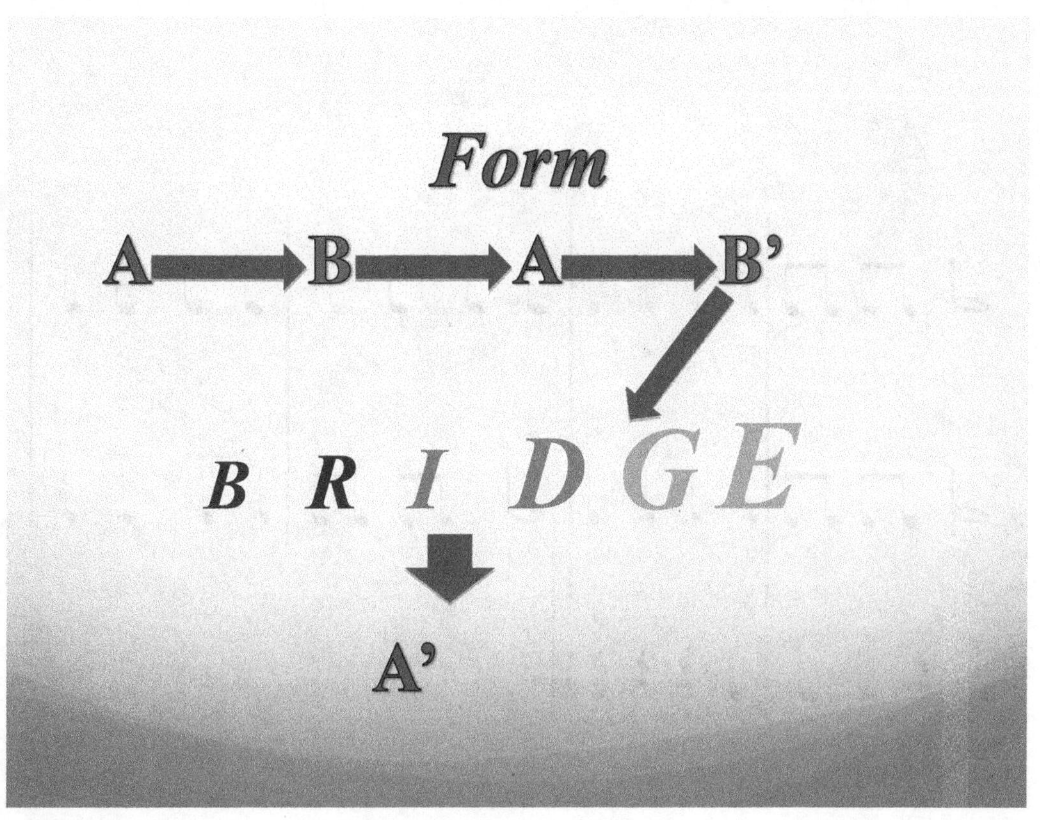

FIGURE 14.6 Listening Experience 14, Slide 6

FIGURE 14.7 Listening Experience 14, Slide 8

FIGURE 14.8 Listening Experience 14, Slide 10

– As an extension, students can stand and step the rhythms for A, B, B', and A' (without music first). Once they are comfortable, they can step the rhythms for these sections while listening to the music (keeping some type of stationary beat during the bridge). Some addition extension activities include:

* Students clap the rhythm for the A and A' sections and step the rhythms for the B and B' sections and then switch.

* Students split into two groups. One group steps the rhythms for A and A' as the other group steps the rhythms for B and B' and then switch.

15

"FOSSILS" FROM CARNIVAL OF THE ANIMALS

Musical Selection:

"Fossils" from *Carnival of the Animals* by Camille Saint-Saëns (performed by Charles Dutoit and the Orchestre Symphonique De Montreal, 1992 Decca)

Tonality (by section):

The A section of the piece is in G Minor. Sections B and C move between B-flat and E-flat Major.

Meter:

This piece is notated in Cut Time (2/2). Since the tempo makes it easy to read these rhythms as if it was in Simple Duple Meter (2/4 or 4/4), I have chosen to notate this using the quarter note as the beat. A teacher could easily convert this back to cut time if he or she wished for the students to experience this with the half note as the beat.

Musical Concepts Experienced/Addressed:

1. Rhythmic Reading (Quarter Note, Two Eighth Notes, Four Sixteenth Notes, One Eighth Note–Two Sixteenth Notes)
2. Rondo Form

Musical Skills/Behaviors:

1. Creating beat-related movements for specific formal sections of the piece
2. Performing rhythmic patterns (reading from notation) for sections of the piece
3. Responding to the form through movement

Age Level:

The rhythmic material would make this more appropriate for upper elementary students (4th–6th grades).

Suggested Procedures:

- Students warm up by echo-speaking, reading, and improvising patterns that utilize quarter notes, eighth notes, and sixteenth notes (slide 1).
- Students will read and speak the rhythm for the A section of the piece while tapping a beat (slide 2).
- Students will whisper the rhythm to the A section as they pat out the rhythm on their legs (using two fingers).

Echo Me...

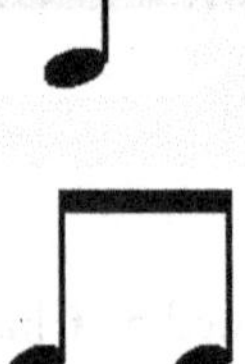

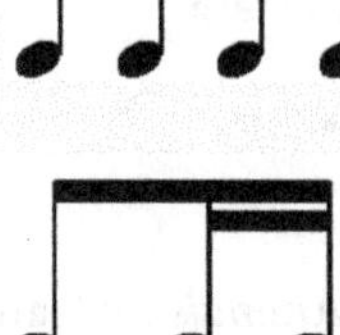

FIGURE 15.1 Listening Experience 15, Slide 1

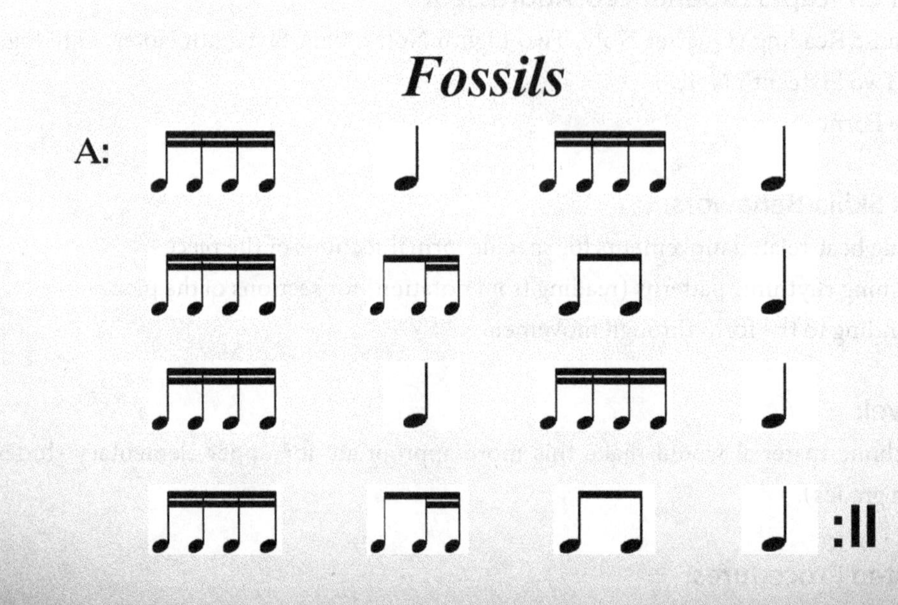

FIGURE 15.2 Listening Experience 15, Slide 2

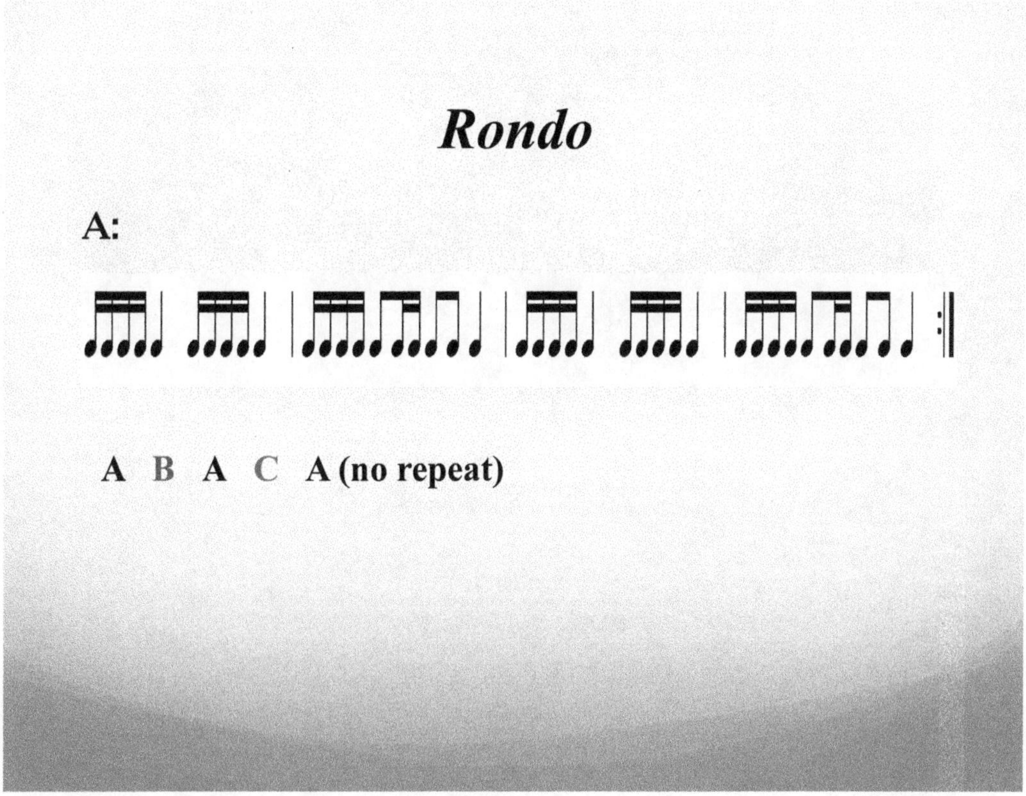

Rondo

A:

A B A C A (no repeat)

FIGURE 15.3 Listening Experience 15, Slide 3

- Students will listen to the A section (0:00–0:17) of the piece as they "play" the rhythm with their fingertips and look at the visual.
- The teacher will show students the form of the entire piece (slide 3).
- Students will find two different ways to move the beat (to use during sections B and C of the music). They will practice these as the teacher keeps the beat with a drum or some other rhythm instrument.
- The students will stand and find space in the room. As they listen, students will stand still and pat the rhythm during the A section of the piece, move the beat one way for section B, and move to the beat a different way for section C. The form of the piece is:
  * A (0:00–0:17)
  * B (0:17–0:33)
  * A (0:33–0:49)
  * C (0:50–1:05)
  * A (1:05–1:14)—for this final section, the A theme is not repeated
- Students will name the form of the piece (Rondo) and define what characterizes this form (a section of music that repeats and contrasting sections of music between each of these repetitions).

16

"HOE-DOWN" FROM *RODEO*

LISTENING EXPERIENCE 16

Musical Selection:

"Hoe-Down" from *Rodeo* by Aaron Copland (performed by JoAnn Falletta and the Buffalo Philharmonic Orchestra, 2006, Naxos American Classics)

Tonality:

D Major

Meter:

Simple Duple (2/4)

Musical Concepts Experienced/Addressed:

1. Rhythmic Reading (Quarter Note, Two Eighth Notes, Four Sixteenth Notes, Eighth Note–Two Sixteenth Notes, Two Sixteenth Notes–One Eighth Note)
2. Form

Musical Skills/Behaviors:

1. Creating beat-related movements for specific formal sections of the piece
2. Performing rhythmic patterns (reading from notation) for sections of the piece
3. Responding to the form through movement

Age Level:

The rhythmic content of this piece, combined with the form and the movement directions, would make this more appropriate for an upper elementary situation (5th–6th grades).

Suggested Procedures:

- Students warm up by reviewing sixteenth note rhythmic patterns through echo-speaking and reading selected patterns (slides 1 and 2):
- After reading the rhythmic patterns on slide 2, the teacher will identify this as the rhythm of the fiddle tune "Bonaparte's Retreat," which is one of the main melodies utilized in "Hoe-Down."
- Students will conduct and speak again as they view slide 3. At the bottom of slide three is a visual indicating how the sections of "Bonaparte's Retreat" are used during the first section of "Hoe-Down" (The brown arrow represents an interlude before the next section of music).

Echo Me...

FIGURE 16.1 Listening Experience 16, Slide 1

Now Read This!

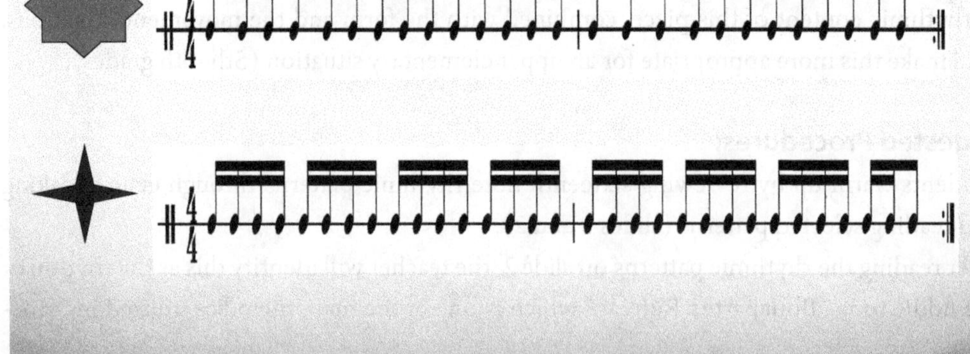

FIGURE 16.2 Listening Experience 16, Slide 2

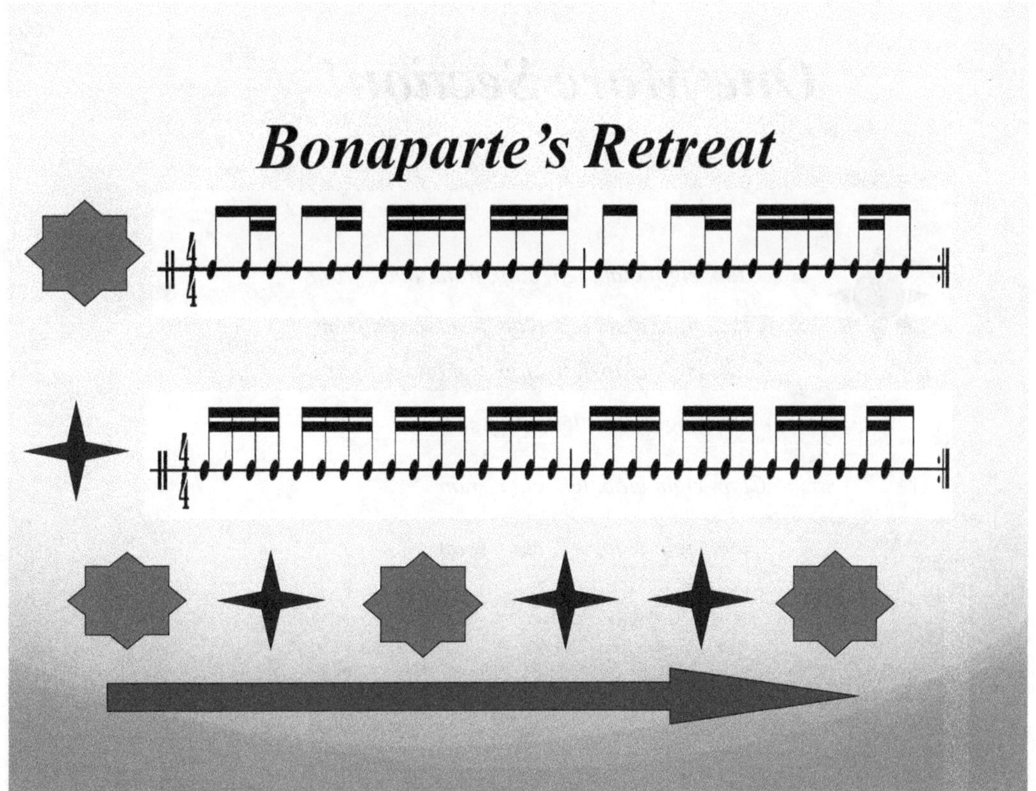

FIGURE 16.3 Listening Experience 16, Slide 3

- Students will listen to this segment of the piece (0:37–1:32) as they conduct and view the visual.
- Students will view a visual of the form and create a contra dance (facing partners in a longways set) that accompanies this section of the music. One example of how this might look is:

Red Star Segment:

* Use the first 8 beats to do a one-hand turn with your partner and trade places.
* Use the second group of 8 beats to do a one-hand turn with your partner and return to your original place.

Blue Star Segment:

* Use the first 8 beats to do the following movements with your partner:
pat-pat-clap-clap (beats 1–4); trade places with a two-hand turn (beats 5–8)
* Use the second 8 beats to do the same motion, but return to original places during the last 4 beats.

- Students will perform the dance with the "Bonaparte's Retreat" section of the piece (0:37–1:32).
- Students will now prepare a dance for the entire piece. The teacher will first address the beginning of the piece and have students view slide 4.
- Students will speak the directions (one word per beat) and then speak and perform the corresponding movements seated with this segment of music (0:16–0:37). An example of this is can be seen on the video "Hoe-Down."

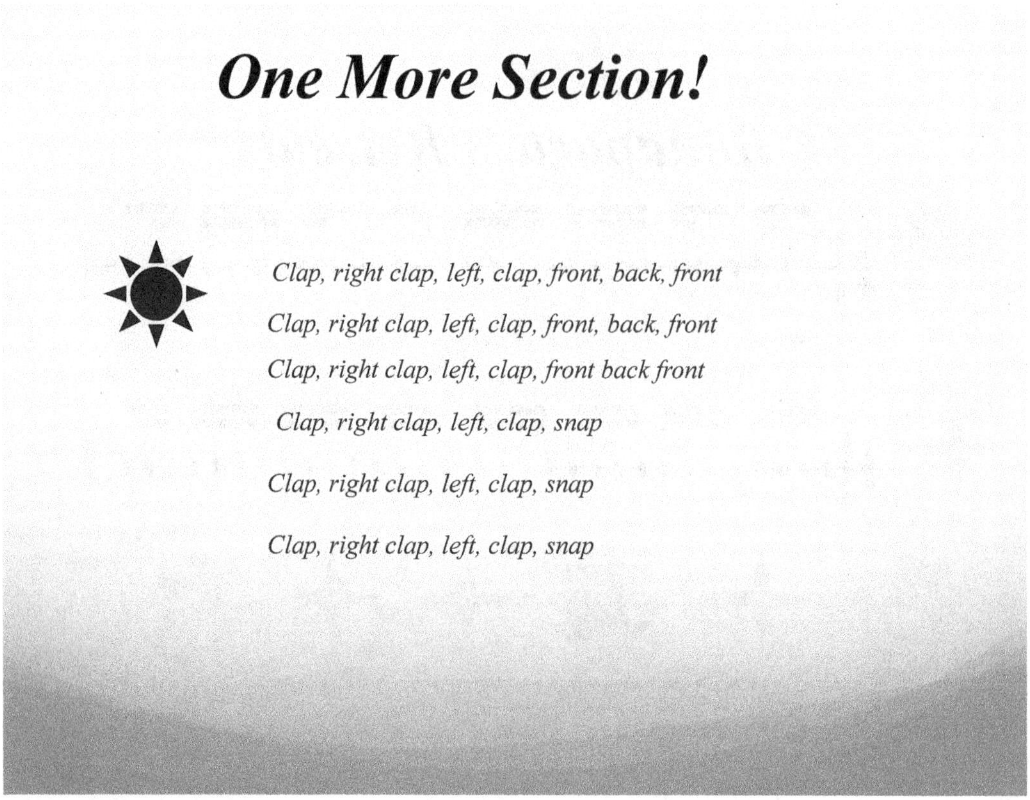

One More Section!

Clap, right clap, left, clap, front, back, front

Clap, right clap, left, clap, front, back, front

Clap, right clap, left, clap, front back front

Clap, right clap, left, clap, snap

Clap, right clap, left, clap, snap

Clap, right clap, left, clap, snap

FIGURE 16.4 Listening Experience 16, Slide 4

Create a Dance!

plus 8

FIGURE 16.5 Listening Experience 16, Slide 5

- Students will get back into their longways set (facing their partners) and perform this segment again with their partner (see the video "Hoe-Down").
- Students view the complete form for "Hoe-Down" on slide 5.
- The teacher will describe the movements for each segment describes the movements:

  Green Sun: perform clapping pattern
  Red Star: perform "Bonaparte's Retreat" movements from above
  Blue Star: perform "Bonaparte's Retreat" movements from above
  Brown Arrow: perform "Bridge Move" (bending knees up and down).
- Students will perform dance with the first half of the piece (0:00–1:32).
- As an extension to this activity, the second section provides students with an opportunity to create their own movements. One possible option is to have students create four 16-beat movements either individually or with a partner (Purple Doughnut, Blue Moon, Blue Heart, Happy Face) that can be performed in the order these appear on the listening map. Another idea would be to create four different groups (Purple Doughnut, Blue Moon, Blue Heart, Happy Face) and have each group create a movement that they perform when their section of music occurs. Each section is 16 beats and the musical order is:

  Purple Doughnut: (1:33–1:40)
  Blue Moon: (1:41–1:48)
  Purple Doughnut: (1:48–1:55)
  Blue Heart: (1:56–2:03)
  Happy Face: (2:03–2:11)
  There is an 8-beat tag at the end of this section (2:11–2:15)

  From 2:17 to 2:43 is another musical interlude in which students will perform the "Bridge move" described previously.

- If students complete this, they are now able to perform the dance with the entire piece. The only difference in the final section of music is that the music that accompanies the Blue Start Movement from "Bonaparte's Retreat" happens one complete time and then adds 8 beats. As a result, students will end up on the opposite side from where they were originally.

"BERCEUSE" FROM *THE FIREBIRD SUITE* 17

LISTENING EXPERIENCE 17

Musical Selection:
"Berceuse" from *The Firebird Suite* by Igor Stravinsky (performed by Jascha Horenstein and the Baden-Baden Radio Symphony Orchestra, 2014, Ameritz Music)

Tonality:
E-flat Minor

Meter:
Simple Duple (4/4)

Musical Concepts Experienced/Addressed:
1. Melody/Minor Tonality
2. Rhythmic Reading (Quarter Note, Two Eighth Notes, Half Note)
3. Form
4. Meter

Musical Skills/Behaviors:
1. Creating movements to correspond with the musical phrases of a specific section of the piece
2. Performing (singing) patterns, a song, and a melodic ostinato in a minor tonality
3. Performing rhythmic patterns (reading from notation)
4. Responding to the meter of the piece through conducting
5. Responding to the form of the piece through movement

Age Level:
The minor tonality would make this activity more appropriate for upper elementary students (5th–6th grades).

Suggested Procedures:
– Students begin by echo-singing minor patterns after the teacher (slide 1).
– Students will listen to, learn, and perform "Hey, Ho, Nobody Home."[1]

[1] Edward Bolkovac and Judith Johnson, eds., *150 Rounds for Singing and Teaching* (New York: Boosey and Hawkes, 1996).

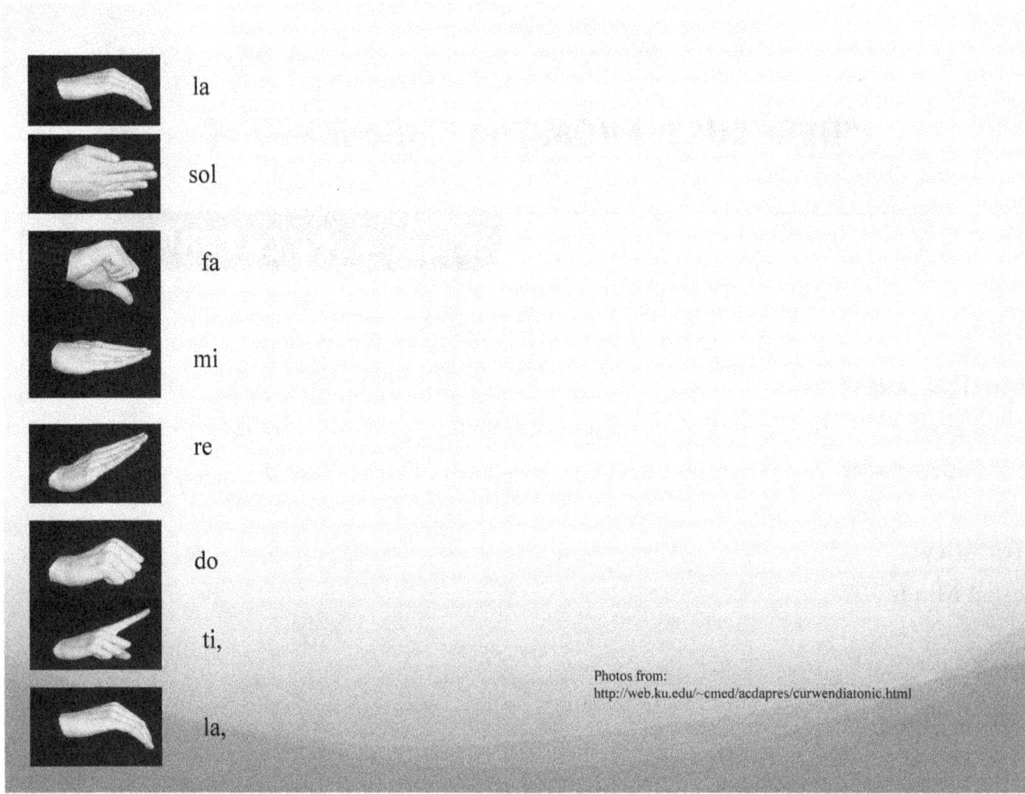

FIGURE 17.1 Listening Experience 17, Slide 1

- Students will perform the song in unison. Once they are successful with this, they will sing and the teacher will enter in canon. Following that, the teacher will sing and students will enter in canon. If students are successful singing in canon with the teacher, they will sing the song in canon with each other.
- The teacher will then sing an ostinato as the class sings the song in unison and then switch parts (the ostinato appears in slides 2 and 3).
- Students will divide into two groups with one singing the ostinato and one singing the melody. Groups will switch and perform again.
- Students will perform as a round with one group singing the ostinato.
- Students will see the rhythm of the ostinato (slide 2). The teacher will ask students to show the contour of the ostinato as they sing and then have them translate and sing the ostinato using solfege (slide 3).
- The teacher will tell students to associate the cloud with this ostinato.
- Students will echo-speak and read various rhythmic patterns. The final pattern will match a rhythmic ostinato (slide 4).
- The teacher will ask students to associate the moon with this second ostinato.
- The students will view a visual representing the form of "Berceuse" (slide 5). They will listen to the piece as they view the visual of the form. The numbers inside each cloud and moon indicate how many times students should perform the melodic or rhythmic ostinati. Each "sun" section contains 16 beats. The following are suggested movements for each section of the piece:

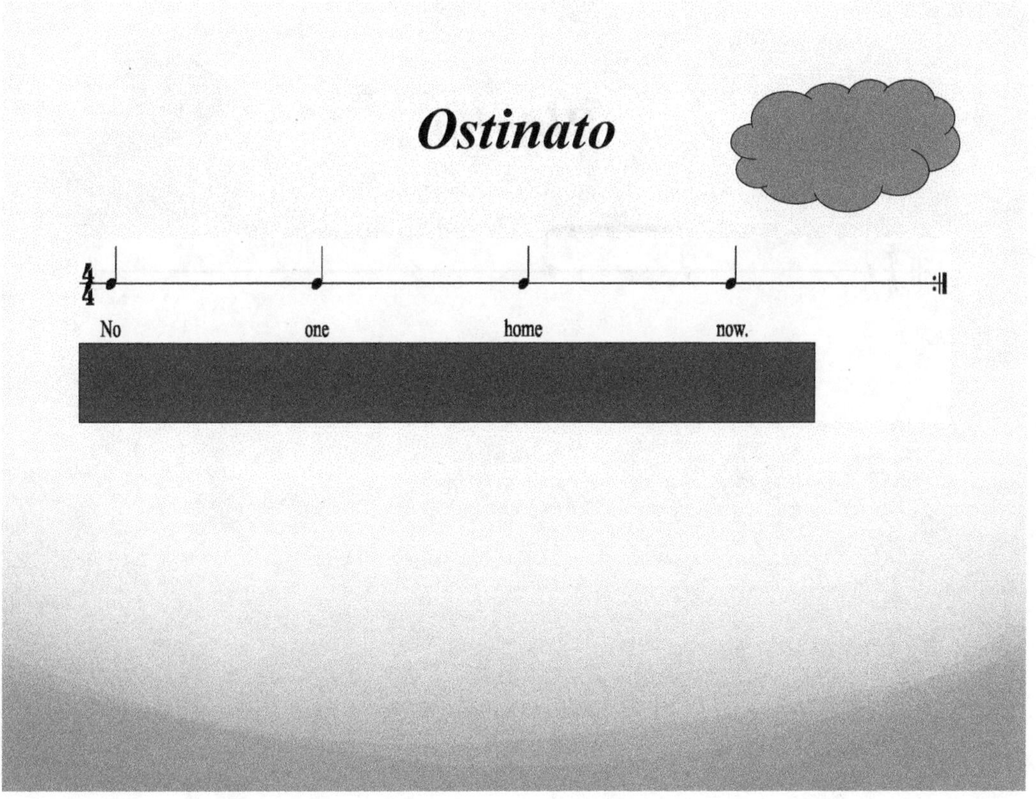

FIGURE 17.2 Listening Experience 17, Slide 2

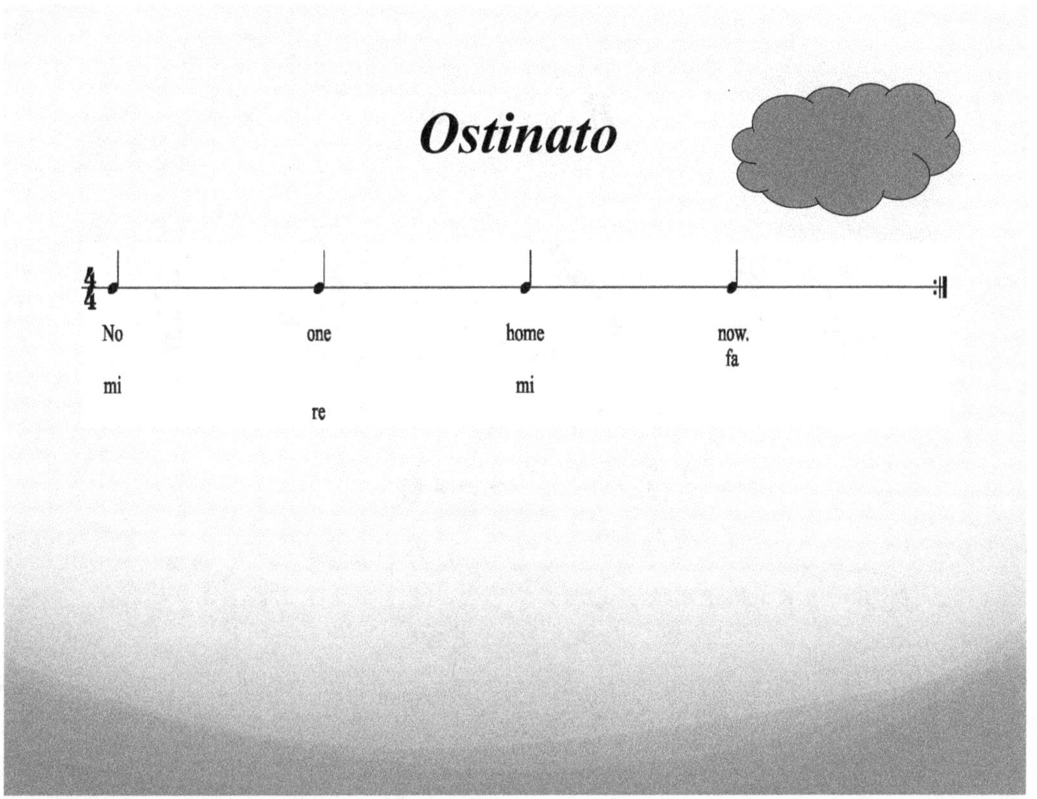

FIGURE 17.3 Listening Experience 17, Slide 3

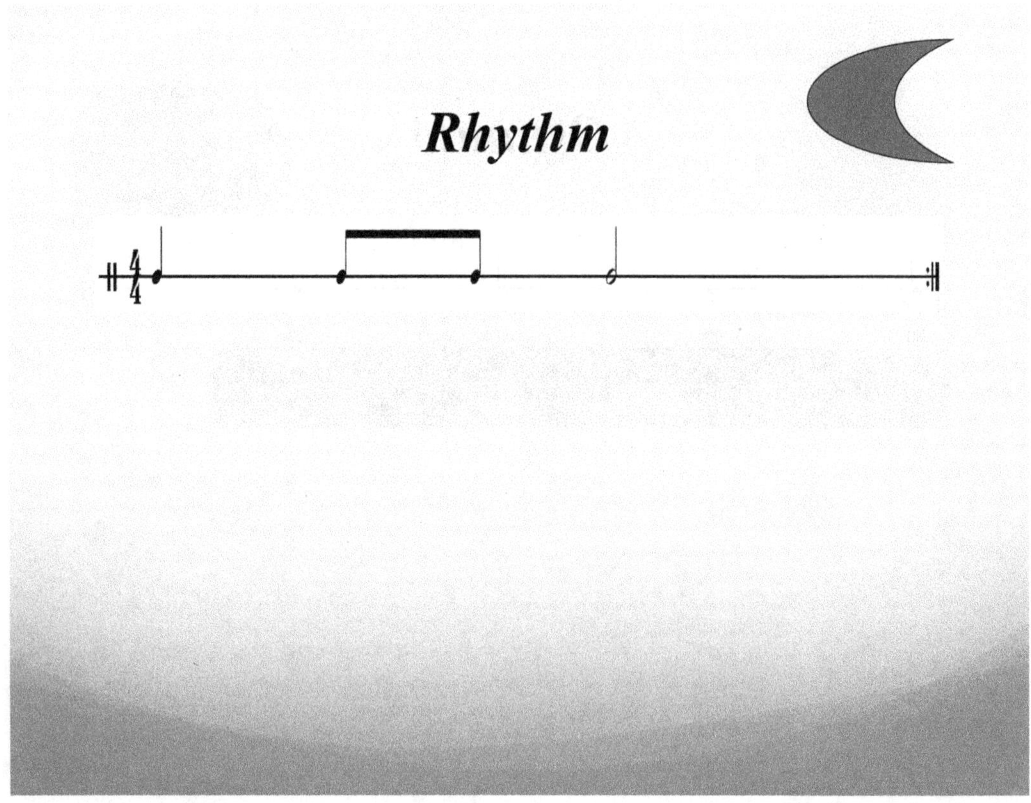

FIGURE 17.4 Listening Experience 17, Slide 4

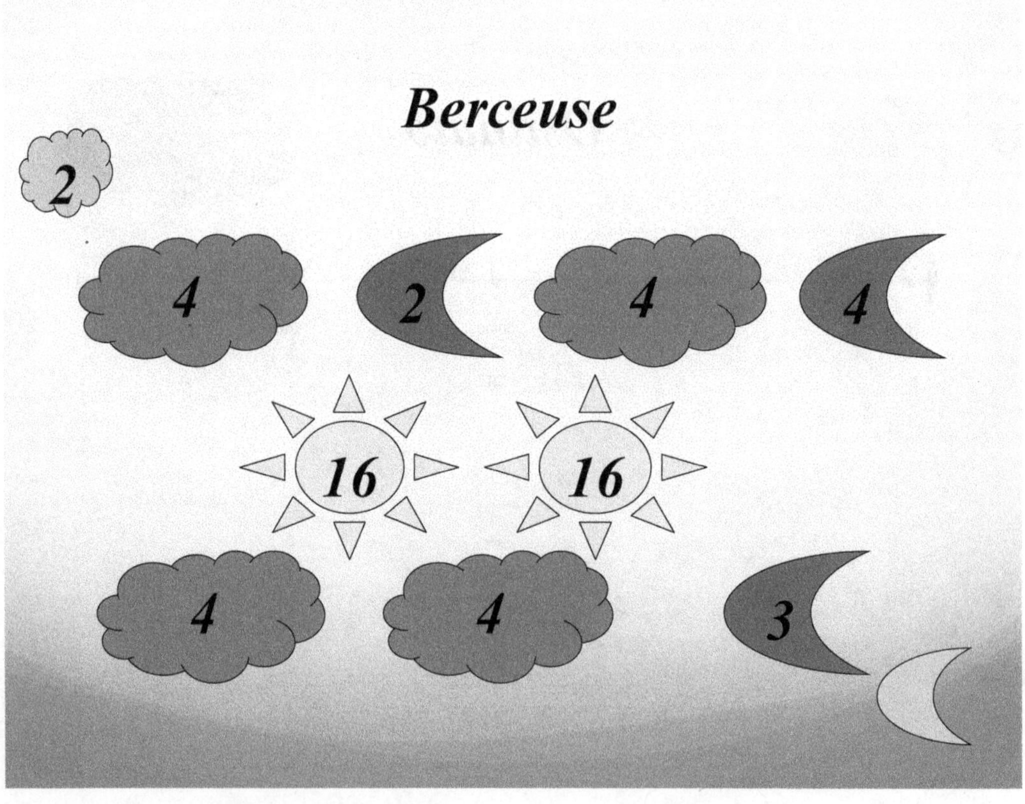

FIGURE 17.5 Listening Experience 17, Slide 5

* Cloud: perform the hand signs for the melodic ostinati
* Moon: tap the rhythm for the ostinati
* Sun: conduct

- The form of the piece is:
  * Introduction (0:00–0:07)—two repetitions of the cloud ositinato
  * A (0:08–0:25)—four repetitions of the cloud ostinato
  * B (0:25–0:35)—two repetitions of the moon ostinato
  * A (0:35–0:52)—four repetitions of the cloud ostinato
  * B (0:52–1:11)—four repetitions of the moon ostinato
  * C (1:11–1:31)—conduct a 4-beat pattern four times (16 beats total)
  * C (1:31-1:50)—conduct a 4-beat pattern four times (16 beats total)
  * A (1:50–2:10)—four repetitions of the cloud ostinato
  * A (2:11–2:28)—four repetitions of the cloud ostinato
  * B (2:29–2:43)—three repetitions of the moon ostinato
  * Coda (2:44–3:36)
- Students will listen again and adapt the movements they utilized to perform as locomotor movements. One possible way to do this would be:
  * Cloud: step the beat and perform handsigns
  * Moon: step the rhythm of the ostinati
  * Sun: draw phrases in the air

OVERTURE TO *RUSLAN AND LYUDMILA* 18

Musical Selection:

Overture to *Ruslan and Lyudmila* by Mikhail Glinka (from *Famous Overtures*, performed by Alfred Scholz and the London Festival Orchestra, 2000, Platinum Disc)

Tonality:

D Major

Meter:

This piece is notated in Cut Time (2/2). Since the tempo makes it easy to read these rhythms as if it was in 2/4 or 4/4, I have chosen to notate this using the quarter note as the beat. A teacher could easily convert this back to cut time if he or she wished students to experience this with the half note as the beat.

Musical Concepts Experienced/Addressed:

1. Rhythmic Reading (Quarter Note, Two Eighth Notes, Half Note, One Dotted Eighth Note–One Sixteenth Note)
2. Form

Musical Skills/Behaviors:

1. Creating movements to perform with specific formal sections of the piece
2. Performing rhythmic patterns (reading from notation)
3. Responding to the form of the piece through movement

Age Level:

The main musical goals of this experience relate to form, so this would be appropriate for upper elementary children (4th–6th grades).

Suggested Procedures:

- The teacher will have students learn the movements to a hand jive first through speaking the text and then by adding movements while speaking the text: pat-pat-clap-clap-cross hands-cross hands-two fists-two fists-thumb out-thumb out (one movement per beat; slide 1). An example of this can be seen on the video *Ruslan and Lyudmila.*

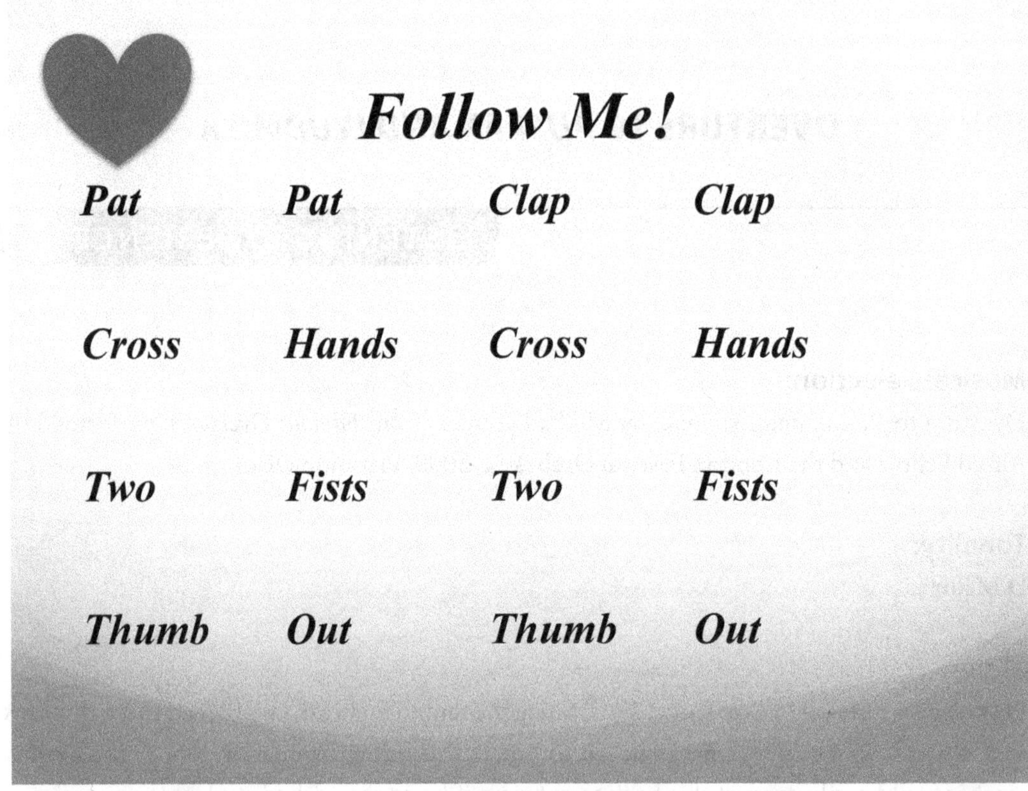

FIGURE 18.1 Listening Experience 18, Slide 1

- The teacher will have students apply the hand jive to the A section of the Overture. Students will listen to A as they perform the hand jive twice (slide 2).
- Since the second half of "A" is slightly different than the first, the teacher will have students create their own 16-beat hand jive that is different from the teacher's. Students will rehearse their movement without the music and then listen to the A section again, performing the first hand jive during the first 16 beats and their new hand jive during the second 16 beats (slide 3).
- Students will stand and form a circle. The teacher will tell students that the B section of the piece also has two parts. For the first part (four measures of 4 beats) students will create a circle dance with two movements (both 8 beats long). For the second part of B (seven measures of 4 beats), the teacher will have students perform a new hand jive: step-step-step-step-pat-pat-pat-pat-clap-clap-clap-clap-cross hands-cross hands-two fists- two fists-thumb out-thumb out-snap (one movement per beat; slide 4). An example of this can be seen on the video *Ruslan and Lyudmila.*
- Students will perform A and B without music and then with the music. The form for the first section of music is:
  * Introduction (0:00–0:15)
  * A (0:16–0:28)
  * B (0:29–0:45)
- The teacher will speak briefly about the plot of the opera based on a Russian folk tale. In it, Ruslan attempts to rescue Lyudmila, the daughter of Prince Vladimir of Kiev, who has been

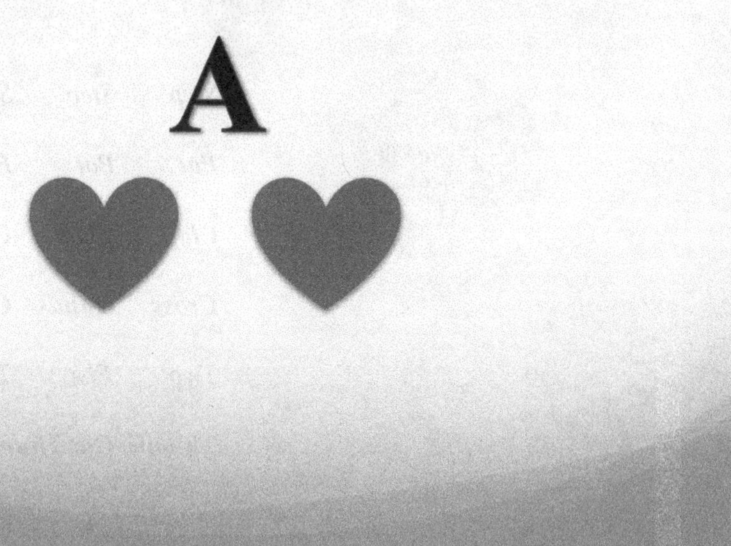

FIGURE 18.2 Listening Experience 18, Slide 2

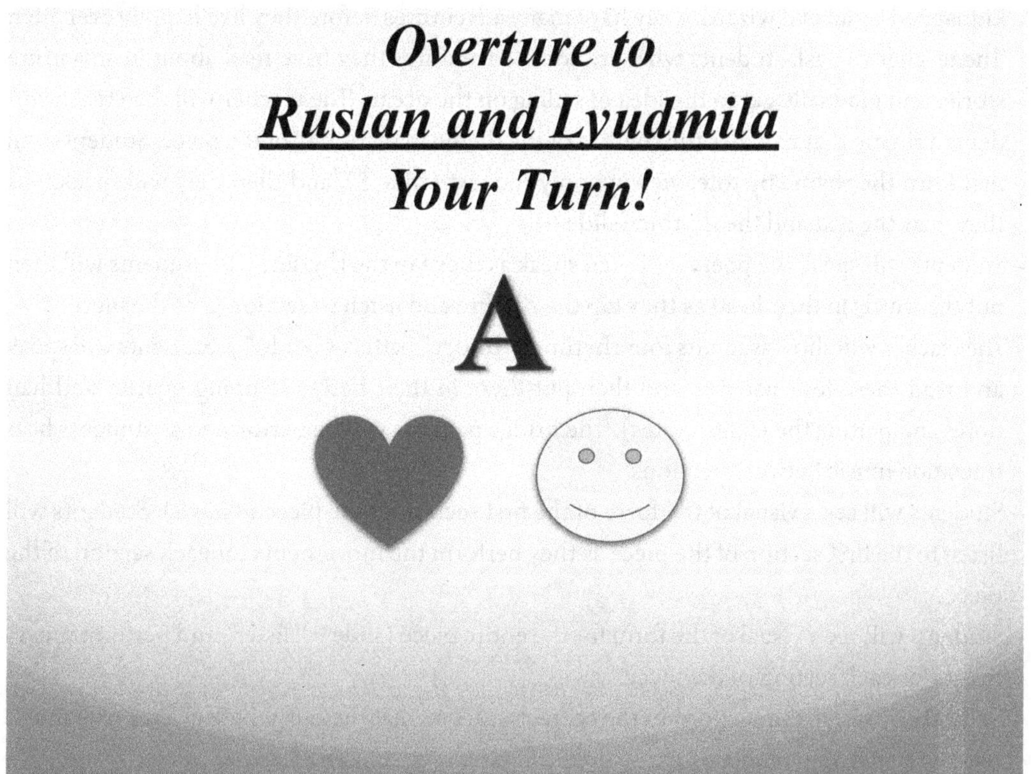

FIGURE 18.3 Listening Experience 18, Slide 3

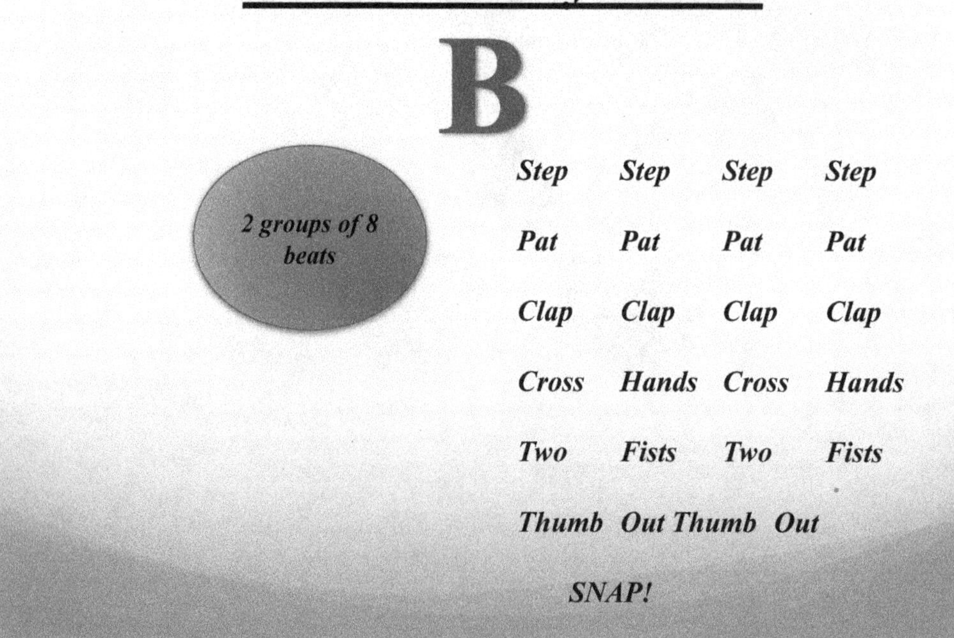

FIGURE 18.4 Listening Experience 18, Slide 4

kidnapped by an evil wizard. They have many adventures before they live happily ever after. The teacher can ask students what are some adventures they have read about in adventure stories and gradually get to the idea of sailing on the ocean. The teacher will then teach students a rhyme that matches the rhythm of the theme in section C of the piece. Students will first learn the rhyme by rote, viewing only the text (slide 5), and then they will speak it as they view the text and the rhythm (slide 6).

- Students will speak the poem and then speak as they tap the rhythm. The students will then put the words in their head as they tap the rhythm and listen to section C of the piece.
- The teacher will show students four rhythmic "bridge" patterns (slide 7). Students will speak and read these four patterns and then put them in their body (stepping quarter and half notes and patting the eighth notes). The bridge patterns will be performed as students hear transition music between sections.
- Students will see a visual of the form of the first section of the piece (slide 8). Students will listen to the first section of the piece as they perform the movements for each section of the piece.
- Students will see a visual of the form for the entire piece (slide 9), listen, and perform movements for each section of the piece.
- Slides 10–18 have the sections in the correct order so that these can be viewed as the music plays to remind students of what to do during each section. The form is:
  * Introduction (0:00–0:15)
  * A (0:16–0:28)—two hand jives

Overture to Ruslan and Lyudmila

C

Sail, we love to sail,
We love to sail away on the ocean!
Sail, we love to sail,
We love to sail away on the ocean!
Sailing to a new adventure,
Waves come crashing down upon us as we venture!
Sail, we love to sail,
We love to sail away on the ocean!
Sail, we love to sail,
We love to sail away on the sea!

FIGURE 18.5 Listening Experience 18, Slide 5

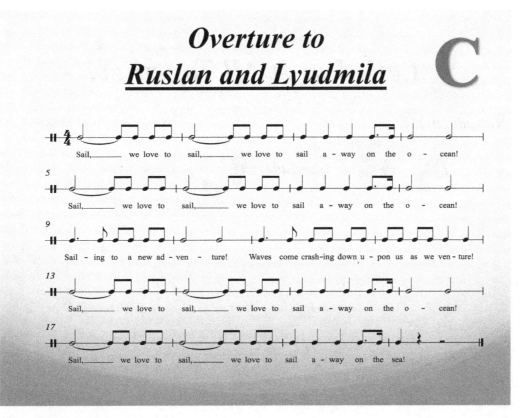

FIGURE 18.6 Listening Experience 18, Slide 6

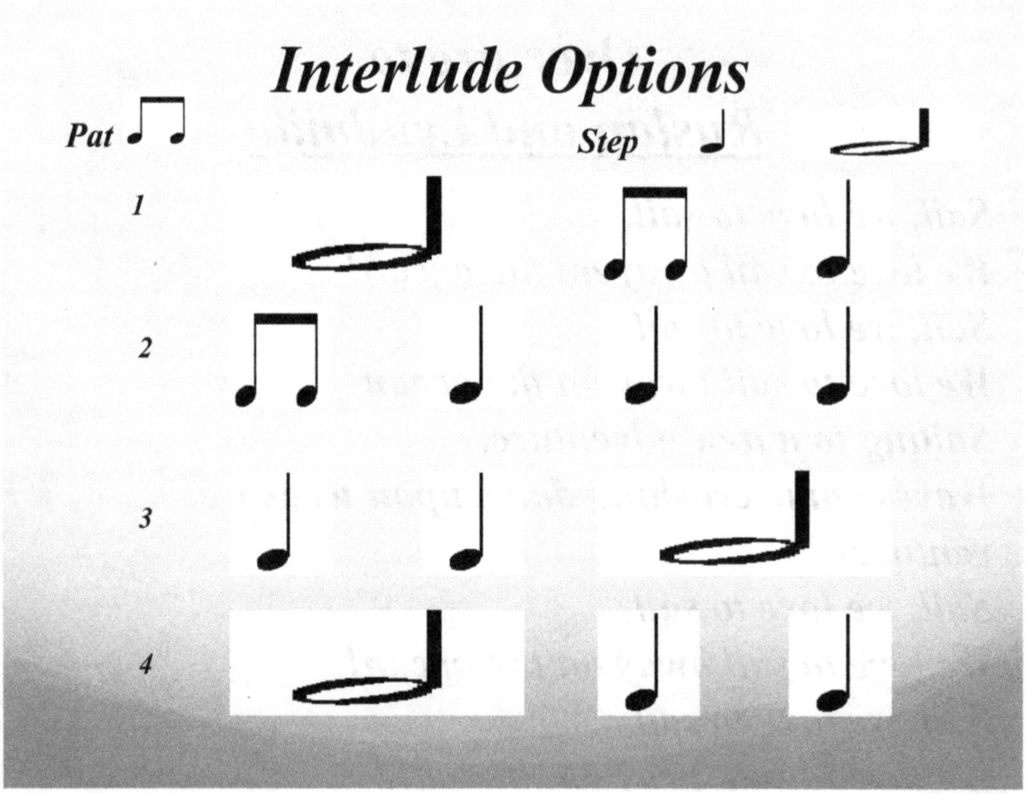

Interlude Options

Pat *Step*

1

2

3

4

FIGURE 18.7 Listening Experience 18, Slide 7

Let's Put It All Together!

Introduction

A B *Interlude* **C**

FIGURE 18.8 Listening Experience 18, Slide 8

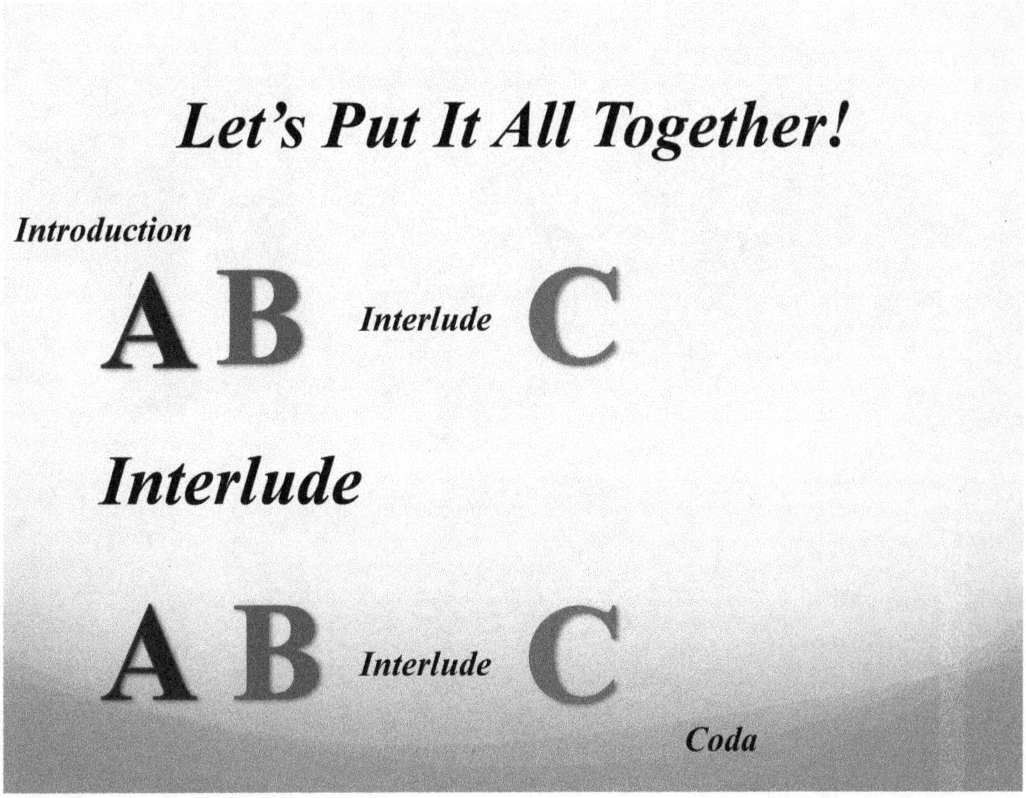

FIGURE 18.9 Listening Experience 18, Slide 9

* B (0:29–0:45)—circle movement plus hand jive #3
* Interlude (0:46–1:03)—move rhythmic patterns
* C (1:04–1:35)—tap the rhythm of the poem and whisper words
* Interlude (1:35–3:10)—move rhythmic patterns
* A (3:11–3:23)—two hand jives
* B (3:23–3:41)—circle movement plus hand jive #3
* Interlude (3:42–4:00)—move rhythmic patterns
* C (4:00–4:31)—tap the rhythm of the poem and whisper words
* Coda (4:31–5:28)—students can conduct using a 4-beat pattern during this section

"ECCE GRATUM" FROM *CARMINA BURANA* 19*

LISTENING EXPERIENCE 19

Musical Selection:

"Ecce Gratum" from *Carmina Burana* by Carl Orff (performed by James Levine, the Chicago Symphony Chorus, and the Chicago Symphony Orchestra, 1985, Deutsche Grammaphon)

Tonality:

F Major

Meter:

Simple Duple (4/4)

Musical Concepts Experienced/Addressed:

1. Melody/Major Tonality
2. Rhythmic Reading (Quarter Note, Two Eighth Notes, Quarter Rest, Half Note)
3. Form

Musical Skills/Behaviors:

1. Creating movements to perform with specific formal sections of the piece
2. Performing (singing) melodic patterns, a melodic ostinato, and the melody of one section of the piece
3. Responding to the form of the piece through movement

Age Level:

The incorporation of singing, reading, and movement would make this more appropriate for upper elementary students (5th–6th grades).

Suggested Procedures:

- Students echo-sing melodic patterns using an extended do hexachord (slide 1).
- Students will recognize and sing "Liza Jane."[1]
- Students will sing the song and add the ostinato found on slide 2. Students will learn and sing the ostinato by rote, not yet viewing the slide.

---

* A demonstration of this entire lesson can be seen on the video ""Ecce Gratum.""

[1] Peter Erdei and Katalin Komlos , eds., *150 American Folk Songs to Sing, Read, and Play* (New York: Boosey and Hawkes, 2004).

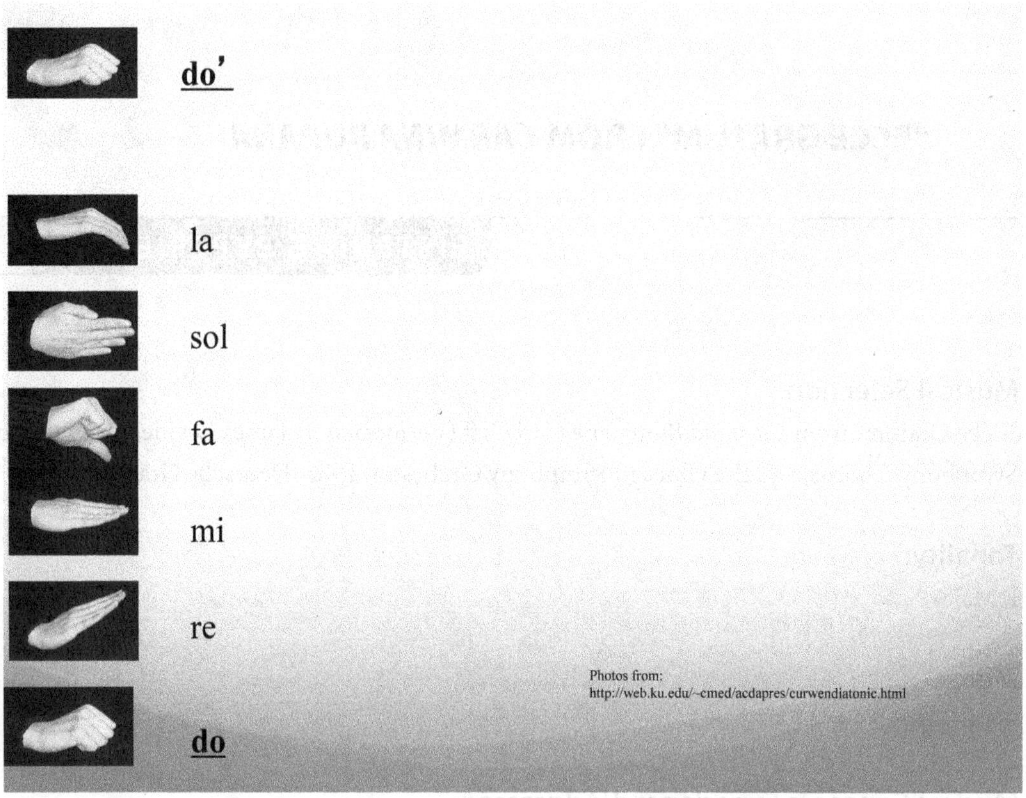

do'

la

sol

fa

mi

re

do

Photos from:
http://web.ku.edu/~cmed/acdapres/curwendiatonic.html

FIGURE 19.1 Listening Experience 19, Slide 1

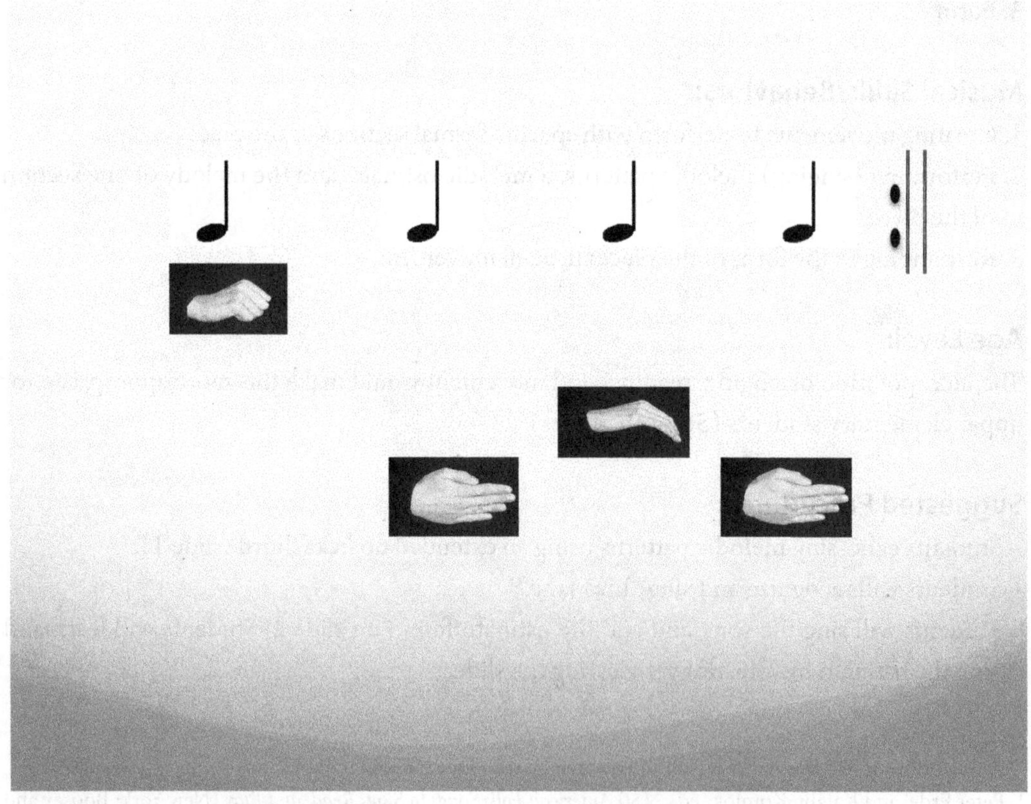

FIGURE 19.2 Listening Experience 19, Slide 2

- Students will determine the contour of the ostinato and then label the solfege, view the ostinato on the slide, and sing the ostinato on solfege.
- The teacher will have students sing the ostinato three times and then add an additional pattern to the end so that they are singing the pattern found on slide 3.
- Students will sing this section as they perform hand signs, and this will be labeled with the orange shape (please see the PowerPoint presentation on the companion website for color versions of the slides). Since this shape appears twice on slide 3, students will have to sing the entire pattern two times.
- Students will review quarter notes, eighth notes, and half notes and speak the rhythm for the second section (cloud) while keeping a beat and then while conducting (slide 4).
- Student will look at the movement directions found on slide 5 for the third section (lightning) of the piece and echo the teacher.
- Students will speak and perform corresponding movements (modeled by the teacher). The movements will be performed to the beat in place: pat (pat lap); clap (clap hands); right and left (right or left hand in front of you as if playing a clapping game with a partner); up down (one hand palm up facing the ceiling and one palm down facing the floor switching positions after two beats).
- Students will view slide 6, showing the form of the entire piece.
- Students will listen to "Ecce Gratum" while performing the movements described for each section: Orange shape (listen and do handsigns for ostinato); Cloud (conducting); Lightning (clapping pattern). During the coda section, students will perform a "rewind"

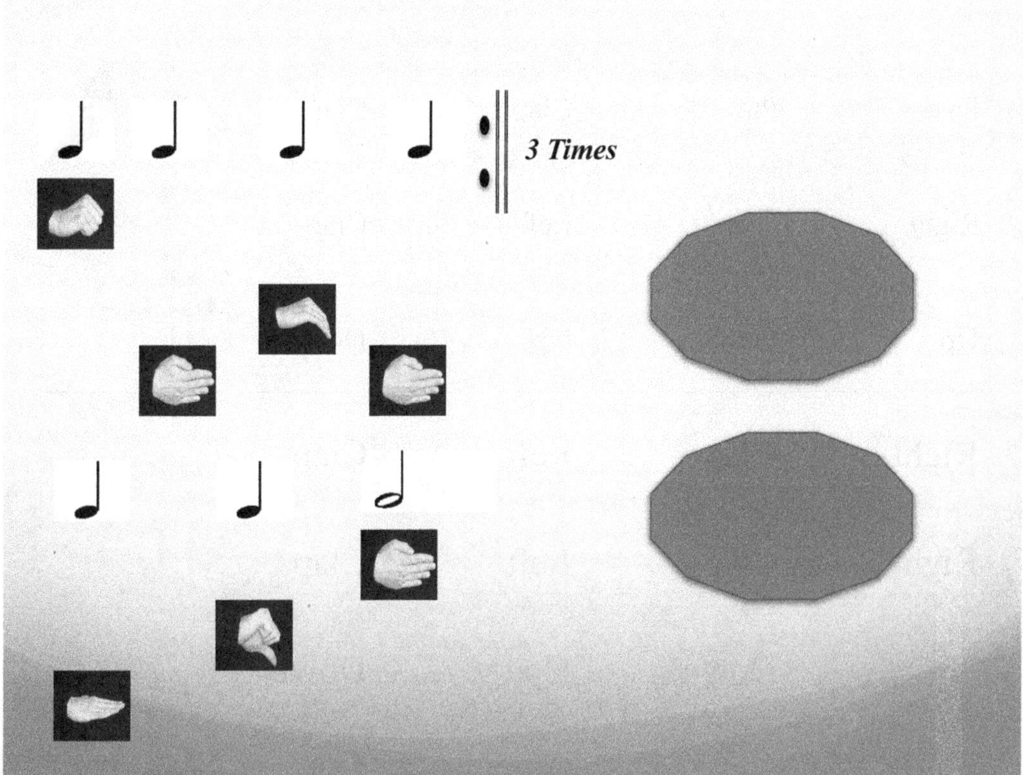

FIGURE 19.3 Listening Experience 19, Slide 3

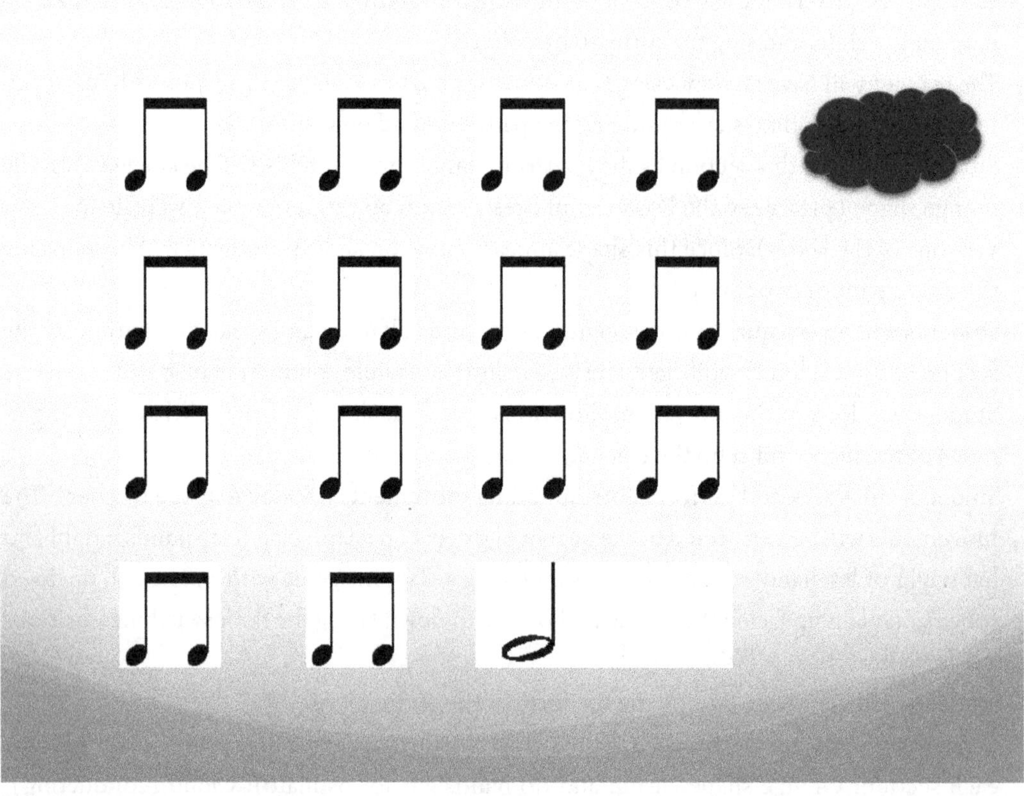

FIGURE 19.4 Listening Experience 19, Slide 4

Pat	Pat	Clap	Clap
Right	Clap	Left	Clap
Up	Down	Up	Down
Right	Clap	Left	Clap
Right	Clap	Left	Clap
Up	Down	Up	Down

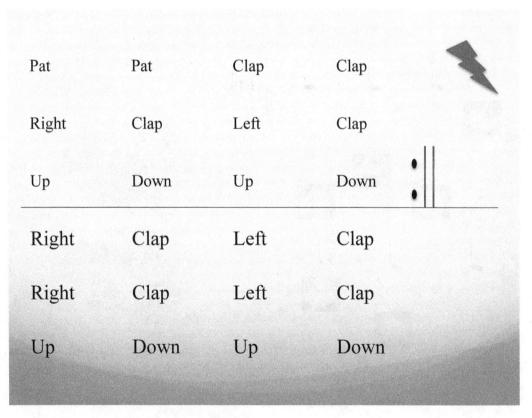

FIGURE 19.5 Listening Experience 19, Slide 5

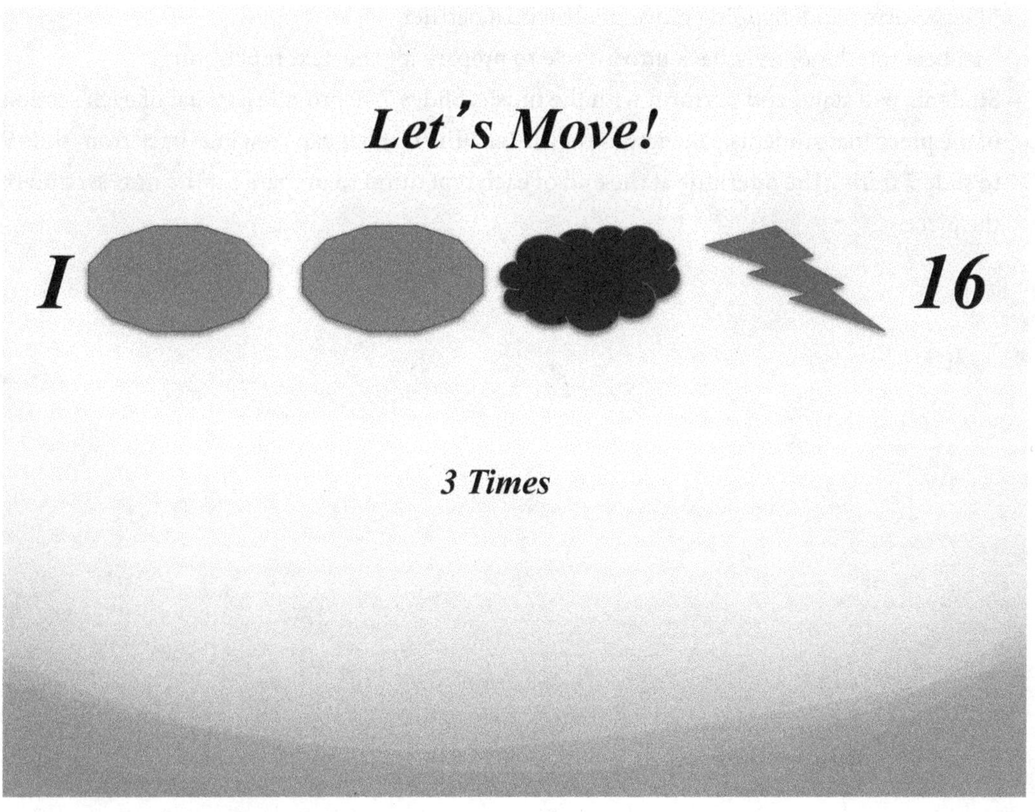

FIGURE 19.6 Listening Experience 19, Slide 6

movement (spinning arms in front of them) to indicate moving back to the beginning of the piece. The form is:
Introduction (I): 0:00–0:06
A (Orange shape): 0:07–0:13
A (Orange shape): 0:14-0:21
B (Cloud): 0:22–0:28
C (Lightning): 0:29–0:44
16-beat interlude: 0:45–0:51
*After doing this once, the piece repeats this form in exactly the same order two more times. Slides 7–9 provide a visual of each section of the piece that students can view as they listen. The teacher can "rewind" back from slide 9 to slide 7 during the interlude at the end of each repetition to prepare for the next section of the piece.

– Students will stand and form a circle. The teacher will guide students in creating a "moving" version of the form, based on the following guides:
* Introduction: stand and listen
* A (Orange shape): some type of circle movement (four groups of 8 beats: a-b-a-b)
* B (Cloud): walk around the room for 16 beats and end up facing a partner

   * C: perform hand-clapping movements with a partner
   * 16-beat interlude: walk back into a circle to prepare for the next repetition
- Students will stand and perform with the music. Slides 7–9 provide a visual of each section of the piece that students can view as they listen. The teacher can "rewind" back from slide 9 to slide 7 during the interlude at the end of each repetition to prepare for the next section of the piece.

20
"ALL YOU NEED IS LOVE"

Musical Selection:
"All You Need is Love" by The Beatles (from *The Beatles 1*, EMI Records Limited, 2011).

Tonality:
G Major

Meter:
Changing between 2/4, 3/4, and 4/4

Musical Concepts Experienced/Addressed:
1. Meter Groupings (2, 3, and 4)
2. Changing Meter

Musical Skills/Behaviors:
1. Performing movements and conducting to the changing meter throughout the piece
2. Responding to the meter of the piece through movement and conducting

Age Level:
The changing meter of the piece would make this a more advanced lesson appropriate for upper elementary students (5th–6th grades).

Suggested Procedures:
(a) Initial Experience:
- Students begin by echoing combinations of words or phrases that utilize two, three, or four syllables (slide 1); e.g., **4** (Partly Cloudy), **3** (Thunderstorm), **2** (Sunshine).
- Students will view the icons for each word/phrase and speak the patterns created by putting the icons together. (As an extension, students can create their own phrases using the icons.)

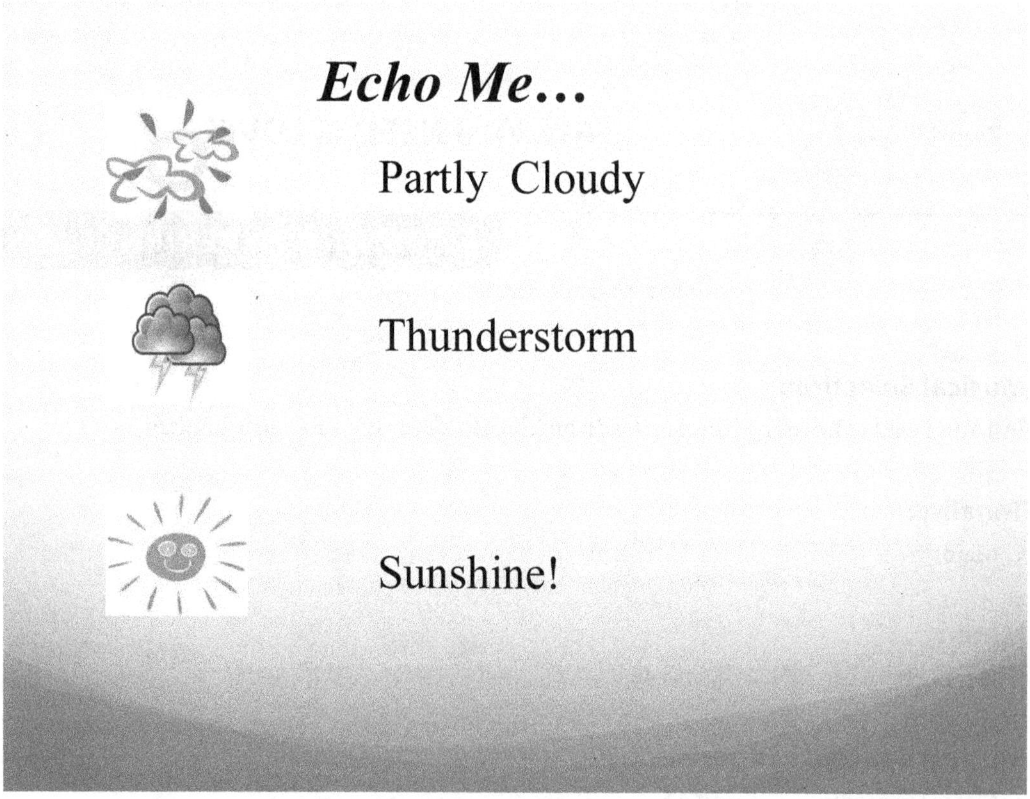

Echo Me...

Partly Cloudy

Thunderstorm

Sunshine!

FIGURE 20.1 Listening Experience 20, Slide 1

Can You Read These and Move?

FIGURE 20.2 Listening Experience 20, Slide 2

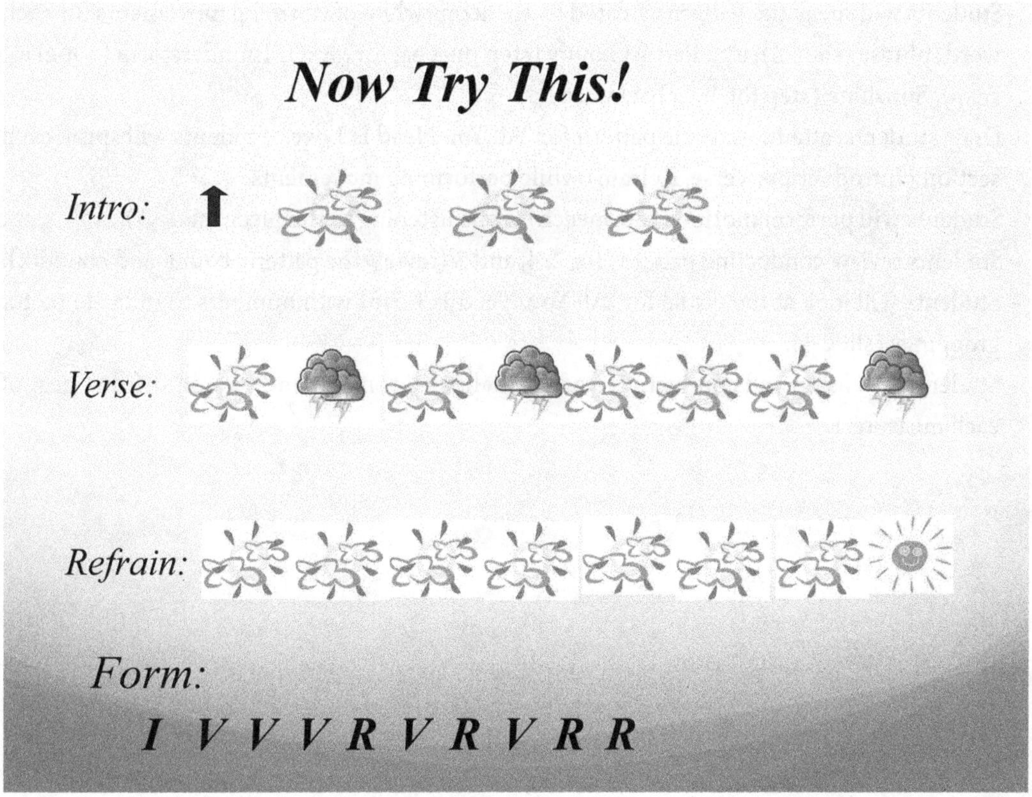

Now Try This!

Intro:

Verse:

Refrain:

Form:

I V V V R V R V R R

FIGURE 20.3 Listening Experience 20, Slide 3

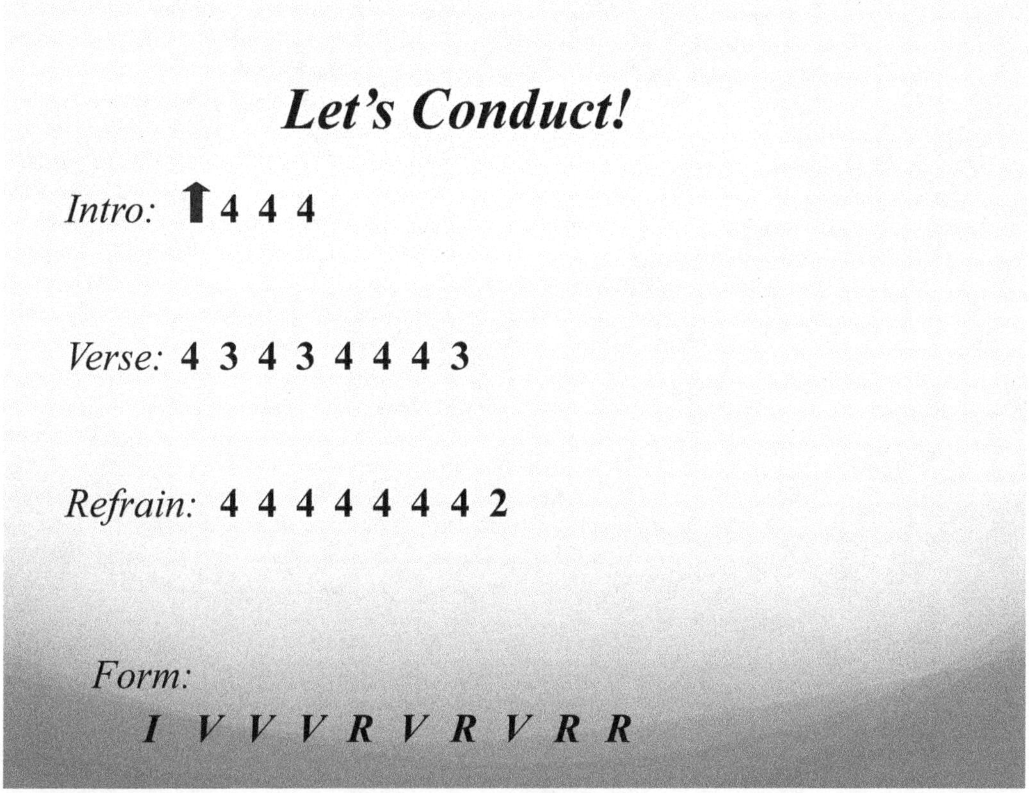

Let's Conduct!

Intro: **4 4 4**

Verse: **4 3 4 3 4 4 4 3**

Refrain: **4 4 4 4 4 4 4 2**

Form:

I V V V R V R V R R

FIGURE 20.4 Listening Experience 20, Slide 4

- Students will speak the patterns created by the icons while performing movements for each word/phrase (slide 2); e.g., Partly Cloudy (step the beat forward), Thunderstorm (pat-clap-snap), Sunshine (step the beat backward).
- Draw students' attention to the pattern for "All You Need Is Love." Students will speak each section (Introduction, Verse, Refrain) while performing movements.
- Students will perform motions (no speech) while listening to the piece (slide 3).
- Students review conducting patterns for 2, 4, and 3 (review the pattern, count, and conduct).
- Students will look at the visual for "All You Need Is Love" with numbers to indicate meter groupings (slide 4).
- Students will listen and conduct. (To add a challenge, conduct and step on the first beat of each measure.)

"UNSQUARE DANCE" 21

LISTENING EXPERIENCE 21

Musical Selection:

"Unsquare Dance" by Dave Brubeck (from *Dave Brubeck's Greatest Hits*, 1996, Sony Entertainment)

Tonality:

A Minor

Meter:

Unusual (7). Given the tempo of the piece, I have chosen to notate this as if it is in 7/8, but the teacher could easily adjust this if he or she prefers to use 7/4 (using quarter note groupings instead of eighth note groupings).

Musical Concepts Experienced/Addressed:

1. Unusual Meter (7)

Musical Skills/Behaviors:

1. Performing movement patterns and conducting patterns corresponding with possible note groupings in 7/8 meter
2. Responding to the meter of the piece through movement and conducting

Age Level:

The meter of the piece would make this a more advanced lesson appropriate for upper elementary students (5th–6th grades).

Suggested Procedures:

- Students will clap two measures of eighth notes in 3/4. Students will then clap as they sing the rhythm/solfege pattern on slide 1.
- The teacher will have students put the first eighth note in each group (marked with an "×") in their laps and all other eighth notes in their hands as they perform.
- The teacher will add one eighth note to the first group of each measure and have students perform again as they view slide 2. Students will sing the same pitch for this eighth note as they do for the other notes in the group.
- The teacher will repeat this process, moving the extra eighth note to the second group (slide 3) and then to the third (slide 4). After performing, students will count the number of eighth notes in each measure to name the meter.

Sing and Perform This Pattern

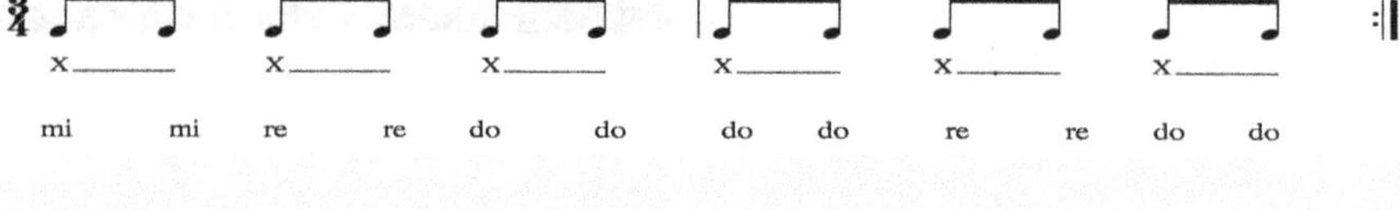

FIGURE 21.1 Listening Experience 21, Slide 1

Now Try This One!

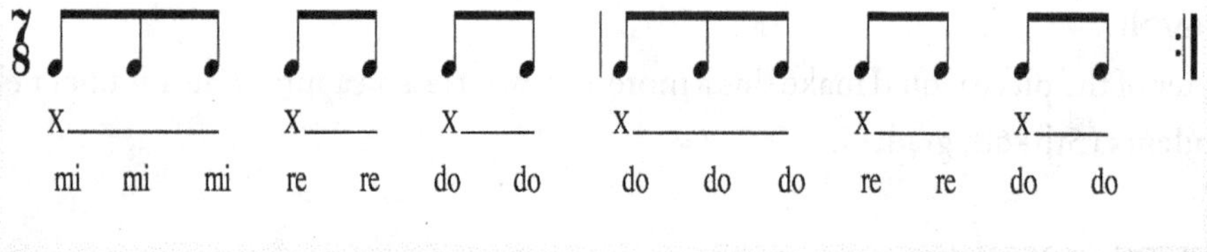

FIGURE 21.2 Listening Experience 21, Slide 2

How About This?

FIGURE 21.3 Listening Experience 21, Slide 3

One More…

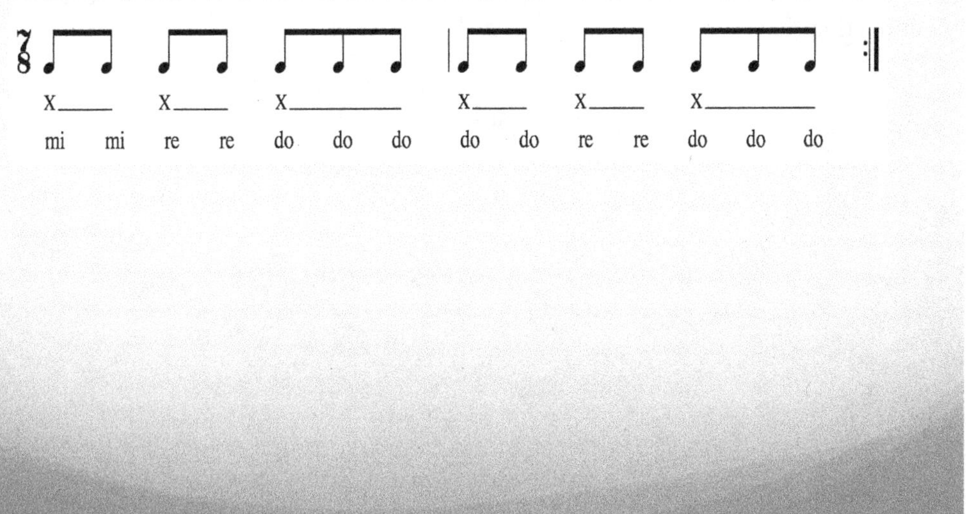

FIGURE 21.4 Listening Experience 21, Slide 4

FIGURE 21.5 Listening Experience 21, Slide 5

- Students will sing the patterns in succession, first with the patting/clapping pattern and then as they step the strong beat of each group.
- Students will sing and conduct each pattern using a 3-beat pattern (one gesture for each group of notes per measure).
- The teacher will remove the solfege and have students view slide 5 as they listen to "Unsquare Dance." Students will determine which of the three patterns is being used.
- Students will listen to the piece again, alternating between the clapping pattern and conducting.

"1234" 22

LISTENING EXPERIENCE 22

Musical Selection:
"1234" by Feist (from *The Reminder,* 2007, Polydor)

Tonality:
D Major

Meter:
Simple Duple (4/4)

Musical Concepts Experienced/Addressed:
1. Melody/Major Tonality
2. Form

Musical Skills/Behaviors:
1. Creating movements to correspond with the form of the piece
2. Performing (singing) melodic ostinato to accompany specific sections of the piece
3. Responding to the form through singing and moving

Age Level:
The melodic ostinati are not difficult. Adding elements such as performing these patterns on instruments or incorporating movement could make the experience more challenging. These options for creativity combined with the genre of music would make this exercise one I would suggest is appropriate for upper elementary students (5th–6th grades).

Suggested Procedures:
- Students begin by echo-singing major solfege patterns as they view slide 1.
- After singing patterns, students will learn three different ostinato patterns. After singing and viewing these separately (slides 2, 3, and 4), students will sing all three one after another (slide 5).
- After singing all three ostinati, the students will view slide 6 (a map of the form of the song).
- Students will listen to the song and sing the ostinato as they appear. In the second segment of the song (row 2 on slide 6), there is a point where students sing one additional fa for 4 beats before moving to the 3rd segment.

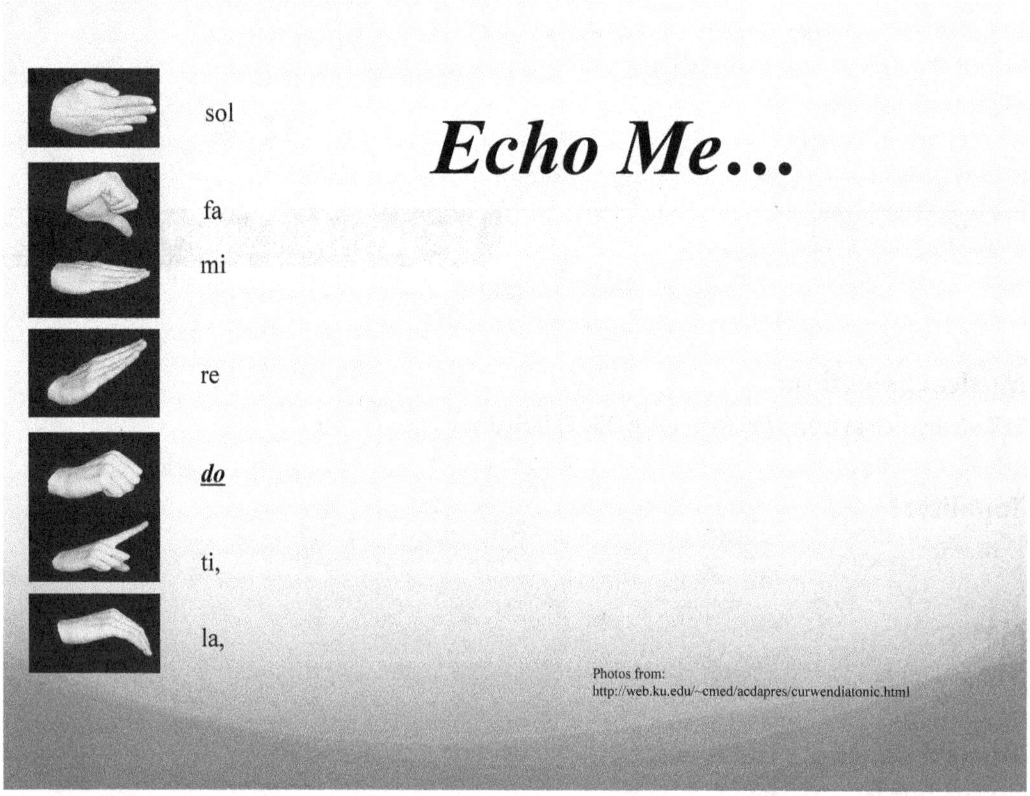

Echo Me...

sol

fa

mi

re

do

ti,

la,

Photos from:
http://web.ku.edu/~cmed/acdapres/curwendiatonic.html

FIGURE 22.1 Listening Experience 22, Slide 1

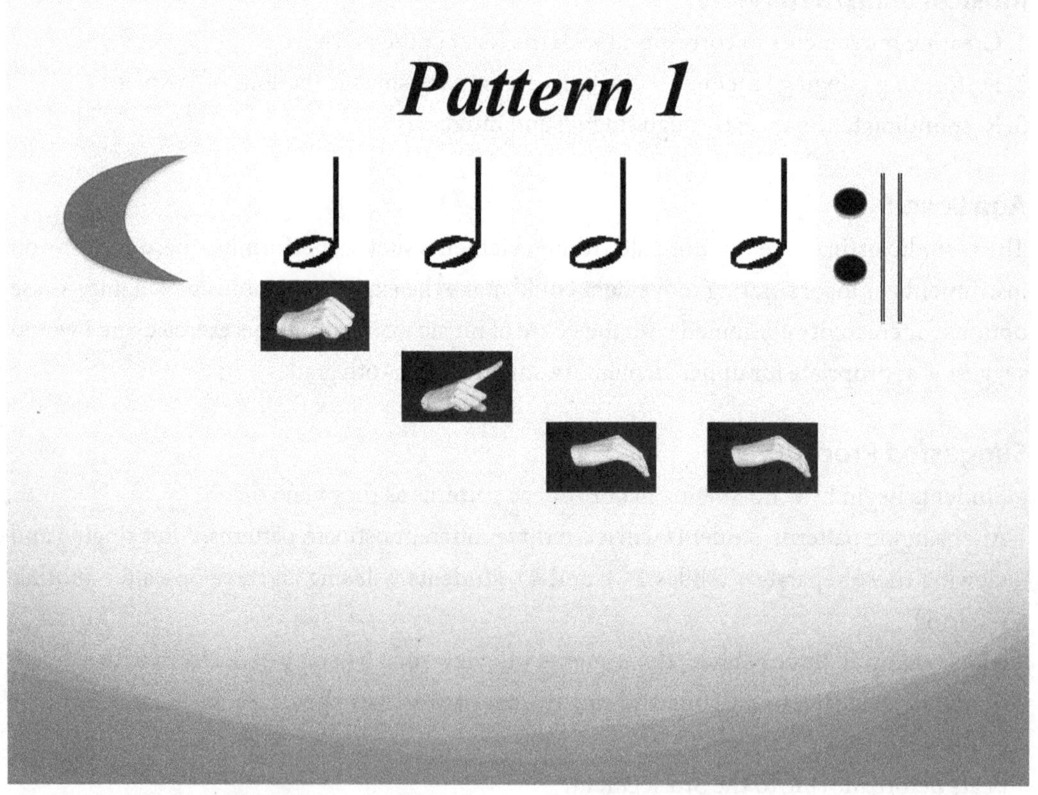

FIGURE 22.2 Listening Experience 22, Slide 2

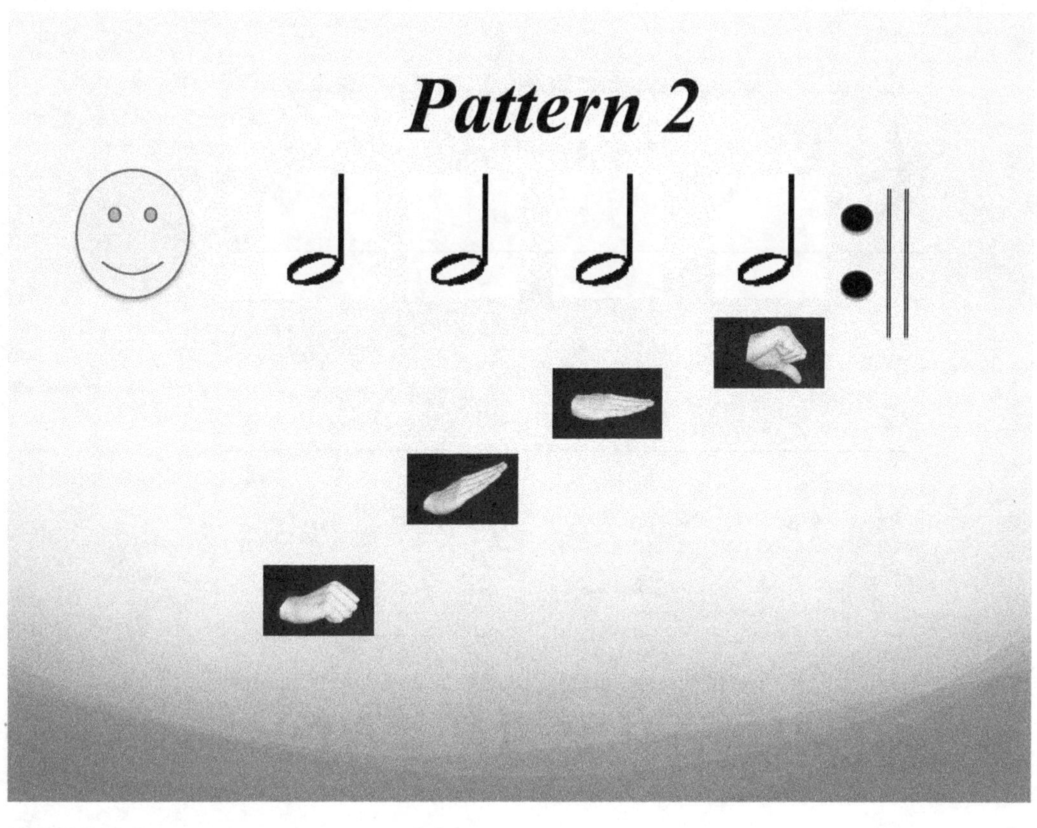

FIGURE 22.3 Listening Experience 22, Slide 3

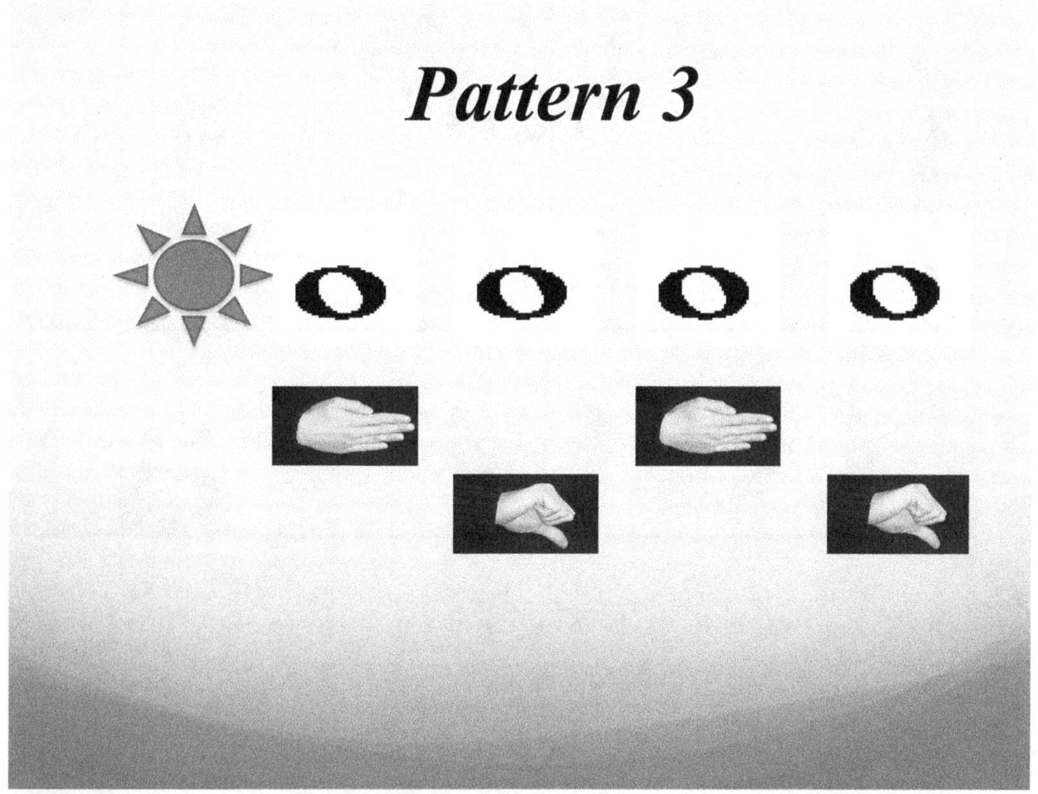

FIGURE 22.4 Listening Experience 22, Slide 4

FIGURE 22.5 Listening Experience 22, Slide 5

FIGURE 22.6 Listening Experience 22, Slide 6

– After students are comfortable singing the ostinati with the recording, there are several extension activities they can add as they listen. Some possible options would include:

*Performing the ostinati on instruments (the song is in D Major).

*Creating movements that correspond with each ostinato pattern and performing these while singing and listening. As inspiration, students can view the video for the song, which contains some wonderful and simple movement ideas (http://www.youtube.com/watch?v=ABYnqp-bxvg).

*Creating movements that correspond with each of the three segments of the song (these correspond with rows 1, 2, and 3 on slide 6).

"E-PRO" 23

LISTENING EXPERIENCE 23

Musical Selection:
"E-Pro" by Beck (from *Guero*, 2005, Geffen)

Tonality:
E Minor

Meter:
Simple Duple

Musical Concepts Experienced/Addressed:
1. Melody/Minor Tonality
2. Reading Melodic Notation
3. Reading Rhythmic Notation (Quarter Note, Two Eighth Notes, Four Sixteenth Notes, One Eighth Note–Two Sixteenth Notes, Two Sixteenth Notes–One Eighth Note)
4. Form

Musical Skills/Behaviors:
1. Creating movements to correspond with the form of the piece
2. Performing (singing and playing recorder) melodic ostinato for specific sections of the piece
3. Performing rhythmic patterns (reading from notation)
4. Responding to the form through singing, playing recorder, and moving

Age Level:
The rhythmic material and use of recorder make this an activity that would be more appropriate for upper elementary students (5th–6th grades).

Suggested Procedures:
- Students begin by singing solfege la-based patterns after the teacher as they view slide 1.
- Students will look at the first ostinato pattern (slide 2) and sing it on solfege. After singing this, the teacher will show students slide 3 (a variation of the pattern that includes an eighth rest). Students will sing the new pattern.
- Students will now view the pattern in staff notation (slide 4). They will sing this on letter names and then play the pattern on recorder. The ostinato should be played a total of eight

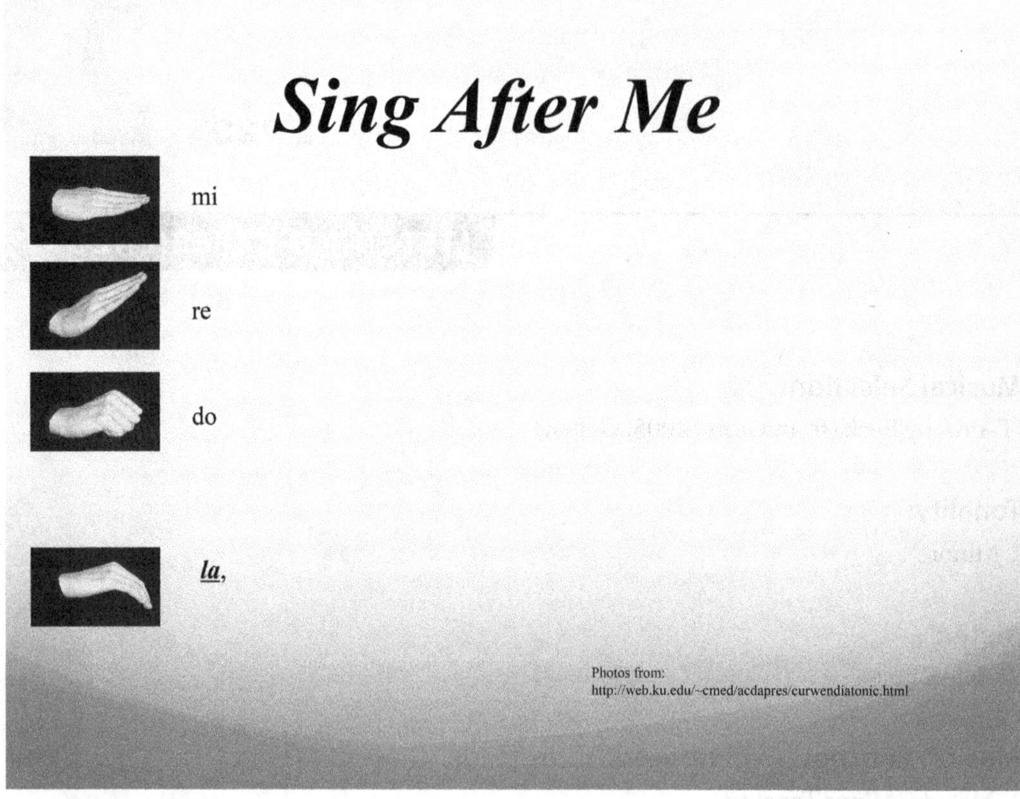

FIGURE 23.1 Listening Experience 23, Slide 1

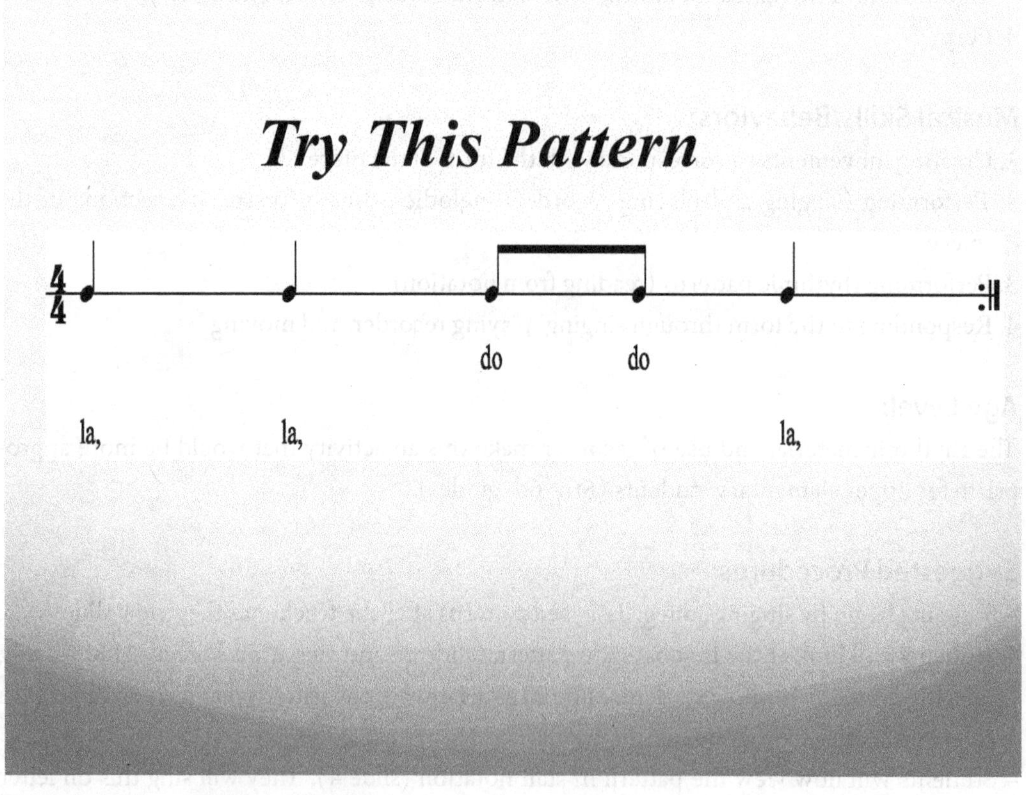

FIGURE 23.2 Listening Experience 23, Slide 2

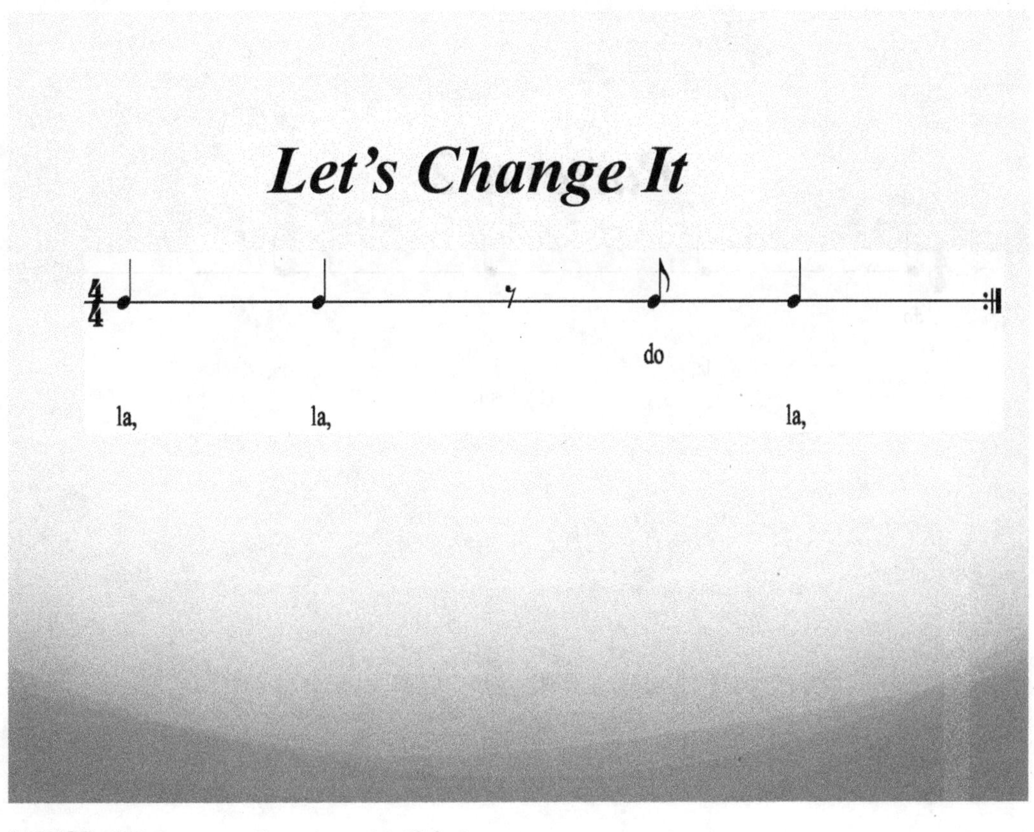

FIGURE 23.3 Listening Experience 23, Slide 3

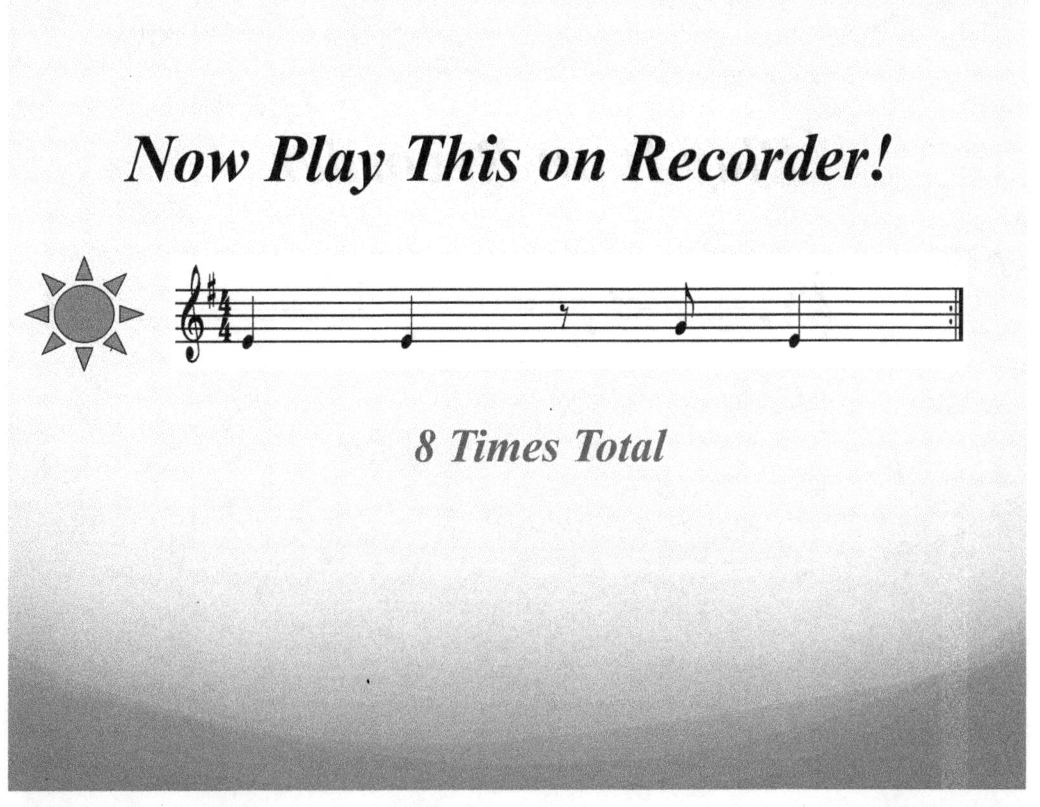

FIGURE 23.4 Listening Experience 23, Slide 4

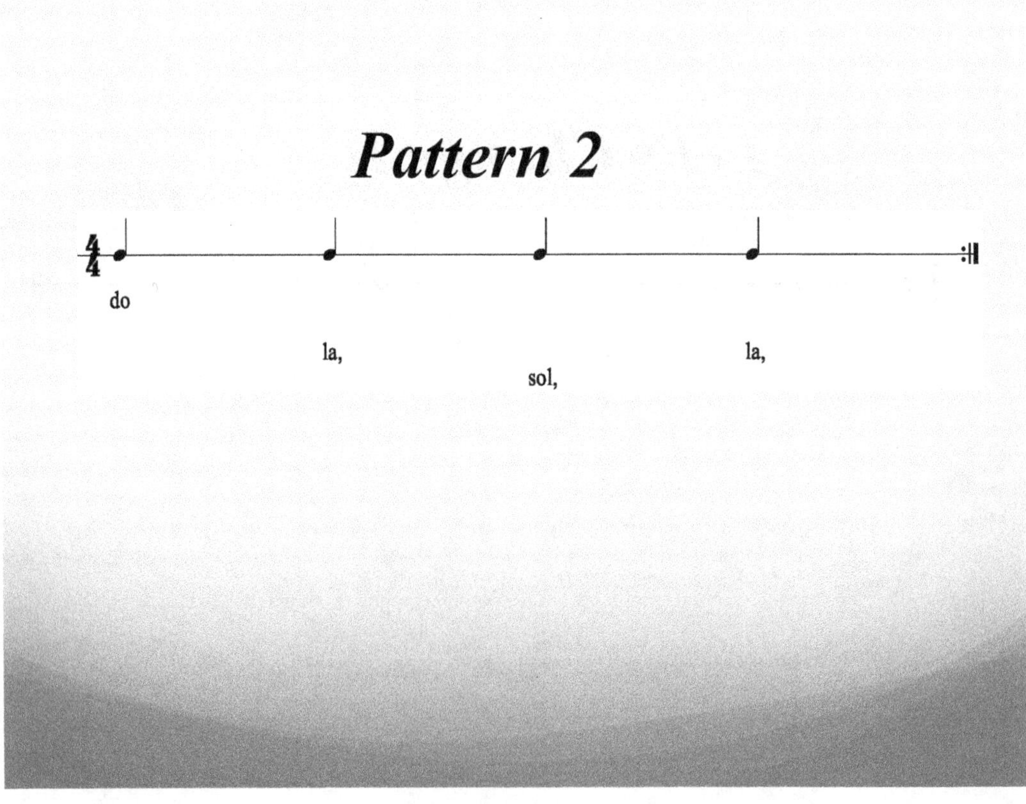

FIGURE 23.5 Listening Experience 23, Slide 5

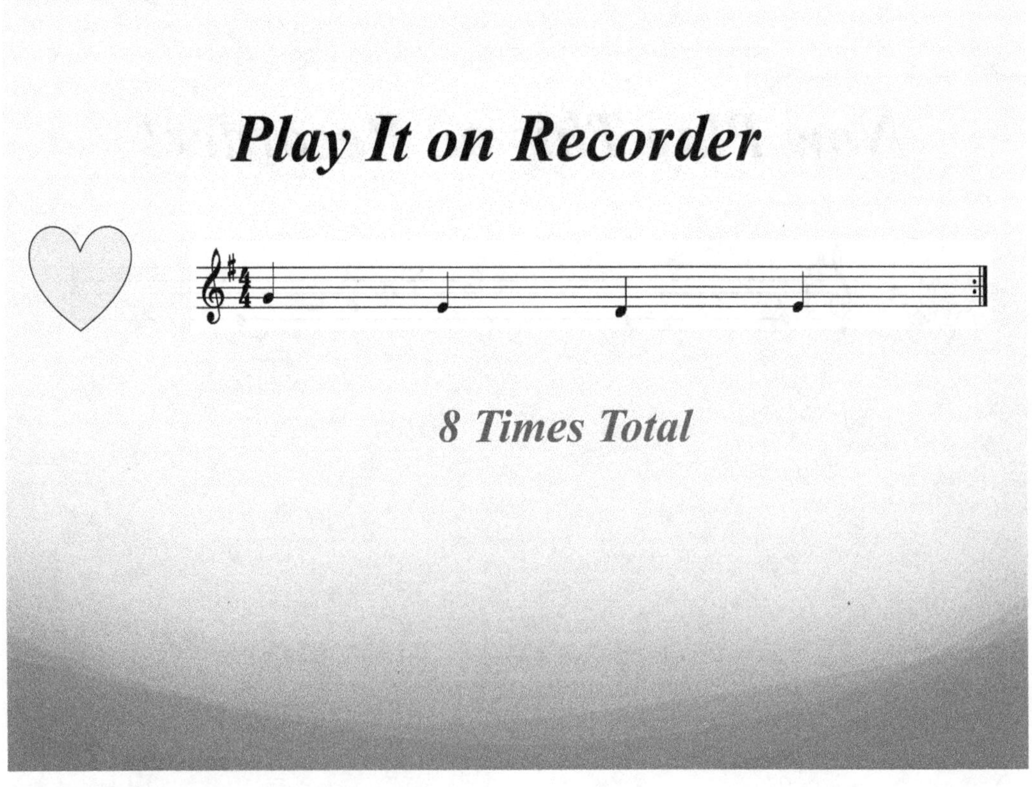

FIGURE 23.6 Listening Experience 23, Slide 6

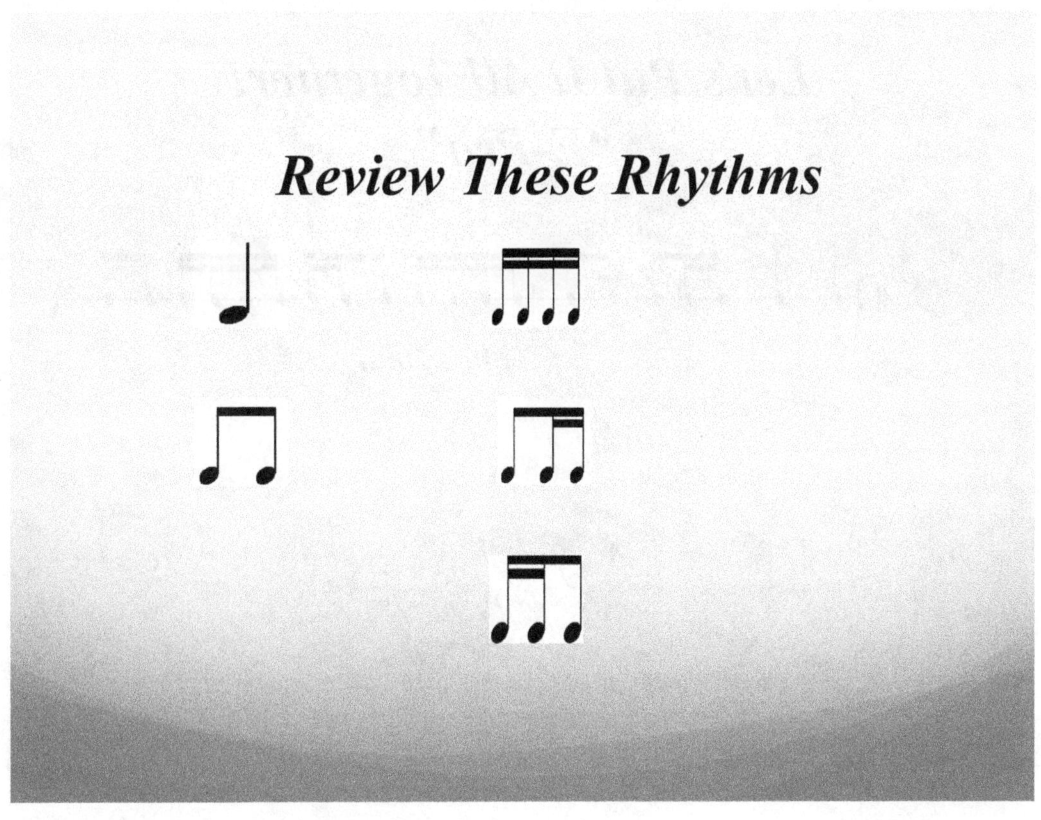

FIGURE 23.7 Listening Experience 23, Slide 7

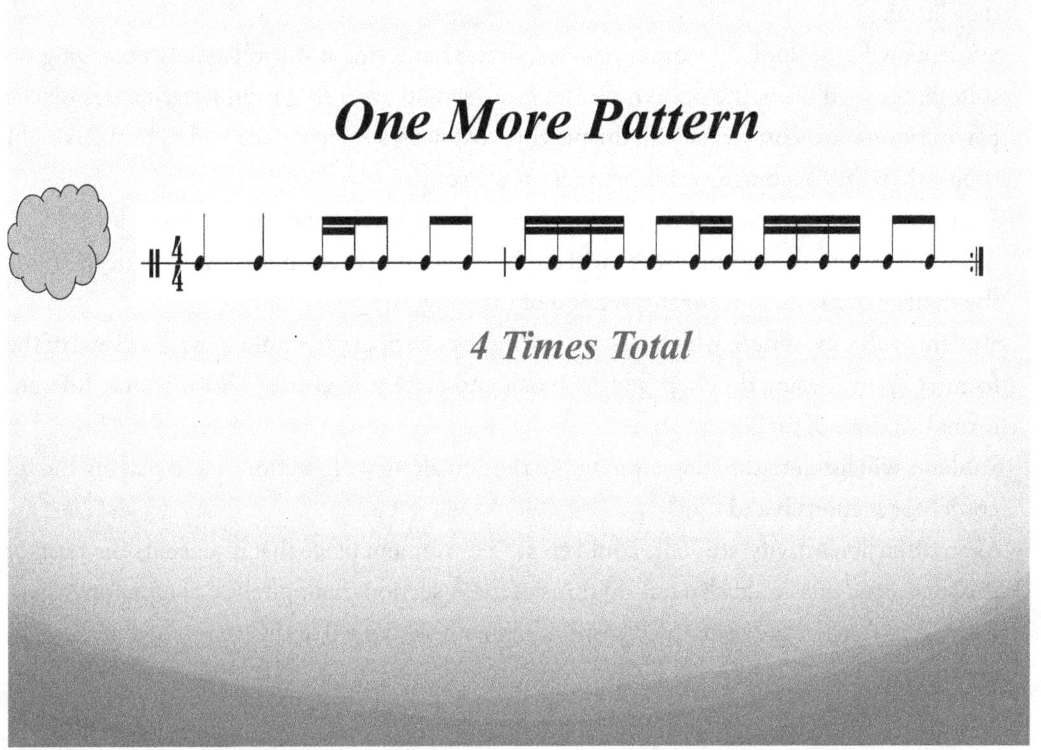

FIGURE 23.8 Listening Experience 23, Slide 8t

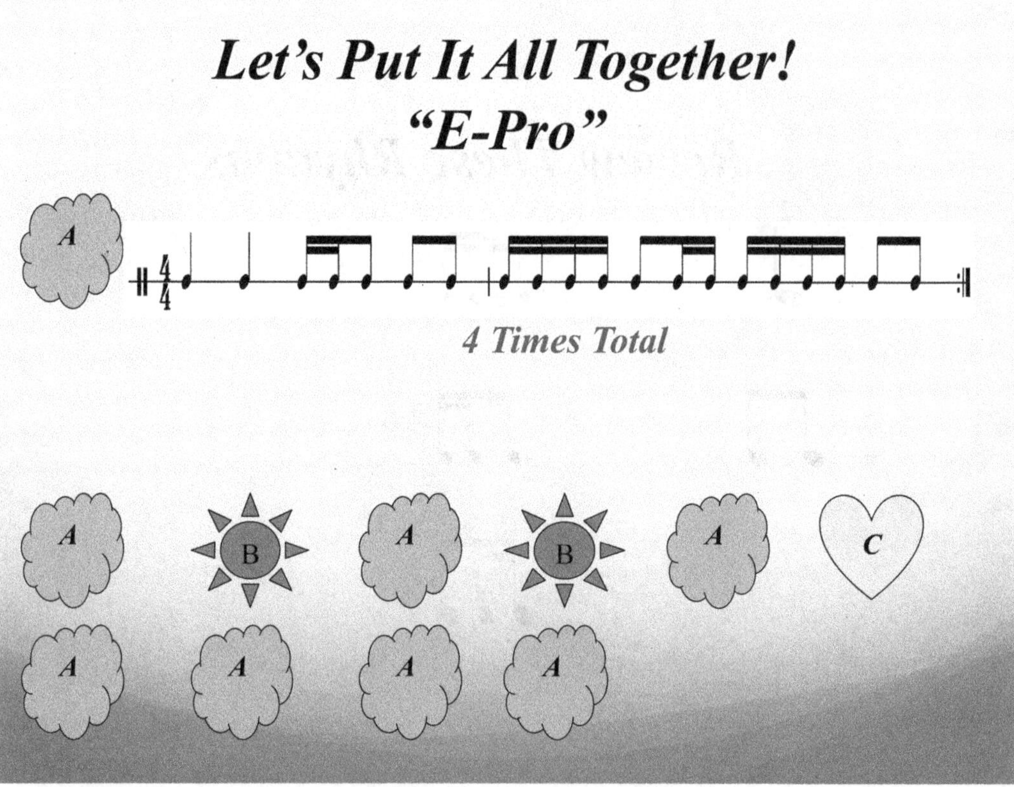

FIGURE 23.9 Listening Experience 23, Slide 9

times in order to correspond with the section of the music students will accompany when they listen.

- Students will now look a second ostinato (slide 5) and sing it on solfege. After singing on solfege, they will view the pattern on the staff (slide 6) and sing it on letter names before playing it on the recorder. As with the previous ostinato, students will need to play this eight times when they accompany this segment of the song.
- Students will review selected rhythmic patterns through echo speaking as they view slide 7. After they review the rhythms, they will apply them to the rhythm pattern on slide 8. This is the rhythm of the melody for this section of the song.
- Students will view slide 9, which has the rhythmic pattern of slide 8 along with a visual of the form of "E-Pro" using the shapes of each ostinato pattern to correspond with the different formal sections of the song.
- Students will listen to the song tapping the rhythm along with section A and playing the recorder for sections B and C.
- As an extension activity, students could create a movement piece that represents the form of the song. Students could also put rhythms of the A section on unpitched percussion instruments and transfer the ostinati corresponding with sections B and C to pitched percussion instruments.

Author's Notes

My interest in creating a book of active listening lessons developed out of the opportunity I had to work with the Discovery Concert program of the Indianapolis Symphony Orchestra. I initially developed sample experiences 8, 9, 10, 11, 12, 13, 14, 16, 17, and 18 as a part of this program. I am indebted to Beth Perdue Outland, Linda Noble, and the ISO for the opportunity to work with them over the past several years.

Special thanks to James F. Daugherty and Erin Stewart from The University of Kansas Vocal/Choral Pedagogy Research Group for the use of the Curwen hand sign visuals on their website in the images on the PowerPoint presentations.

Some of the ideas published in this collection were initially published (in part or whole) in the follow music education journals:

Listening Experience 17 "Berceuse"

Gault, B. "Listen Up!" *Southwestern Musician* (February 2012): 70–72.
Reprinted with permission from the Texas Music Educators Association.

Listening Experience 22 "1234"

Gault, B. "Listen to the Music! Popular Music and Active Listening." *Orff Echo* 43, no. 4 (2011): 10–13.
Reprinted with permission from the American Orff-Schulwerk Association.

Listening Experience 23 "E-Pro"

Gault, B. "Popular Music: Friend or Foe?" *Kodály Envoy* (2006). Copyright © 2006 by OAKE: Organization of American Kodály Educators. Used by permission. No additional use without written permission.
Gault, B. "Common Ground: Finding Commonalities in Diverse Musical Material." *General Music Today* 20, no. 1 (2006): 1–14. Copyright © 2006 by National Association for Music Education. Excerpt reprinted with permission.

About the Author

Brent M. Gault is an associate professor of music education at the Indiana University Jacobs School of Music. His areas of interest include music education policy, children's vocal development, and music listening in childhood. Articles by Gault have appeared in the *Journal of Research in Music Education* and the *Bulletin for the Council of Research in Music Education.* He is the co-editor, along with Carlos Abril, of the book *Teaching General Music: Approaches, Issues, and Viewpoints,* also published by Oxford University Press.

Printed in the USA/Agawam, MA
August 1, 2019

708468.006